CURTIS'S
FLOWER GARDEN
DISPLAYED

CURTIS'S FLOWER GARDEN DISPLAYED

120 PLATES FROM THE YEARS 1787–1807

WITH NEW DESCRIPTIONS BY

Tyler Whittle

AND

Christopher Cook

Oxford New York Toronto Melbourne

OXFORD UNIVERSITY PRESS

1981

Oxford University Press, Walton Street, Oxford OX2 6DP

London Glasgow New York Toronto
Delhi Bombay Calcutta Madras Karachi
Kuala Lumpur Singapore Hong Kong Tokyo
Nairobi Dar es Salaam Cape Town
Melbourne Wellington
and associate companies in
Beirut Berlin Ibadan Mexico City

This edition first published by Oxford University Press 1981
©1979 Text Michael Tyler-Whittle
©1979 Edition Colibri AG, Bern,
ein Tochterunternehmen der Hallwag Verlagsgruppe

British Library Cataloguing in Publication Data
Whittle, Tyler
Curtis's flower garden displayed.
1. Botany – Classification
I. Title II. Cook, Christopher
III. Curtis, William
582   QK95
ISBN 0-19-217715-X

Set by King's English Typesetters Ltd
Printed in Great Britain by
The Thetford Press Ltd
Thetford, Norfolk

CONTENTS

INTRODUCTION

A Note on the Source of the Plates

It is to the imagination and enterprise of a professional botanist that we owe the remarkable plates which are figured in this first volume of *Curtis's Flower Garden Displayed*. William Curtis lived from 1746 to 1799 at a time when a general interest in plants and in botanical exploration showed that western culture had reached a new level. This was chiefly stimulated by Carl von Linné, a Swede whose work on a world-wide survey of the plant kingdom at last took botany into the world of science. Many distinguished botanists had laid paths for him to follow, chief of them a Swiss, Gaspard Bauhin, and an Englishman, John Ray, but it was Linné's systematic methods and the publication of his *Genera Plantarum* and *Species Plantarum* that began to stabilize the naming of plants and thus moved men to travel the globe in the search of new species. His Latinized name, Linnaeus, became a household word in cultured circles all through Europe.

Curtis was born in this Golden Age of botany in Alton, the English town that also claims Jane Austen as a native. He was the son of a Quaker tanner and apprenticed at 14 to his grandfather, the local apothecary. This obliged him to study simples or single plants used for their medical properties, but he was either too idle or too uninterested to learn much until he caught what has been called 'the botanic infection' from a rather unlikely source – the ostler of an inn next to the apothecary's shop. This unusual ostler was not only literate but also a great admirer of the herbals of Gerard and Parkinson in which, though they still have credulous followers, magic and superstition and quackery were well mixed with slipshod botany and horticulture. The apprentice apothecary proved to be a more critical admirer than his cicerone. He studied other books on natural history and went out as a field biologist and made collections of insects and birds' eggs as well as dried plants, and became an expert on birdsong. In the end he was such an enthusiast that plants and birds and insects stole his heart away from the profession that had been chosen for him. In a desultory fashion he worked in London, first as an assistant then as a partner in an apothecary's practice. But he could not find time for both medicine and natural history, sold out to his partner, bought a patch of land to grow plants, and assiduously collected all round London. For a time he was Garden Superintendent and Botanical Demonstrator of the Society of Apothecaries, work which was much more congenial, but after five years he gave it up. He was too energetically concerned with his own interests, writing so much that he became one of the first users of shorthand; publishing a book on insects; translating and illustrating Linnaeus's book on the same subject; and herborizing alone and with friends, which resulted in his *Catalogue of Plants growing wild in the Environ of London*. In 1778 Curtis made a bold move, deciding to have his own botanic garden which would be open to subscribing patrons. Three times he changed its site until he found what he really wanted. By then he had been greatly helped by contributions of plants from several famous gardens and nurseries and he was growing more than six thousand species. These were divided into sections, medicinal, poisonous, culinary, agricultural, British and ornamental plants and shrubs, and the show beds illustrated Linnaeus's system of classification. His really was a botanic garden, not simply a pleasure ground or nursery. The proprietor gave lectures to subscribers on the premises and, for an additional subscription, they were free to take seeds and plants for their own use as and when they became available. In addition to this huge enterprise Curtis was a ceaseless writer, writing his many lectures, and published *A History of the Brown-tail Moth* in an over-sanguine attempt to reassure fruit growers and gardeners who so feared the pest that large rewards were offered for collecting and destroying them, and an excellent work for farmers, *British Grasses*. He almost ruined himself by being over-ambitious and issuing the first part of a lavishly illustrated *Flora Londoniensis*, and he was a long time recovering his fortunes. Nevertheless, as his botanic garden thrived, he conceived another bold idea, to issue a regular magazine for the edification of those who, stimulated by Linnaeus, were eager for more information. It has been joked that in England especially people could 'do botany without botanical names, almost without plants'. William Curtis was quite sure they could not. Even then he hesitated. Plates were prepared and possibly he wrote up the plants, but they were put aside for about a year. It was understandable. The failure of *Flora Londoniensis* had been a sharp lesson. Nevertheless, in February 1787 the first issue of *Curtis's Botanical Magazine* was issued. It proved to be the birth of a botanical and publishing phenomenon.

Right from the beginning Curtis declared his purpose was didactic. He wrote in the first issue that he intended to make a 'Display of the Flower Garden of ornamental Foreign plants cultivated in the open ground, the greenhouse, and the stove'. Each plate was hand-coloured and letterpress described the plant's names, its synonyms used by pre-Linnaean authors, its provenance, its time of flowering, and notes on cultivation. Curtis himself had every qualification to look after the letterpress but, though a skilful draughtsman, he did not feel competent to manage the illustrations. Nevertheless, instead of simply hiring available artists, he took the unusual course of having one specially trained for the purpose, a young man named Sydenham Edwards who turned out to be one of the most brilliant of all plant delineators. Sowerby and Sansom, both talented artists, did some of the work, but only 75 out of the first 1,232 plates. Edwards was the regular artist and did all the others. At first he engraved his own plates on copper; then Sansom became chief engraver. William Graves was the colourist and even after almost two hundred years the colours are still fresh. Only the scarlets and crimsons and some of the whites have suffered, and especially in the copies at the Royal Botanic Gardens at Kew where, until recently, a neighbouring gasworks belched out fumes that did these colours mischief. The Zurich copies, from which the plates in this work are taken, have escaped. Curtis's plan was to issue three plates with letterpress each, and he did this faithfully for the rest of his life. His creation is possibly unique. Though it has had ups and downs and the proprietorship has changed from time to time, the magazine has been in continuous publication ever since. Through some of the most passionate moments of history, through wars and revolutions and assassinations, and through the making and disintegration of great empires, *Curtis's Botanical Magazine* has been regularly issued and may be counted as a token of man's civilization even when he has appeared at his most barbarous. Subscriptions may still be taken out by writing to the Editor, The Royal Botanic Gardens, Kew, Richmond, England.

As first editor Curtis was able to choose his plants arbitrarily from a rich field. This first volume of *Curtis's Flower Garden Displayed* contains 120 plates selected from the first 25 bound volumes of the *Botanical Magazine* produced in the twenty years from 1787 to 1807. They do not appear in Curtis's arbitrary order but, to give the plants a special historical and geographical interest, in the chronological order in which, so far as is known, they were introduced from their original habitat into cultivation. The sole exception to this rule is Plate 80 which belongs chronologically between Plates 75 and 76 but being oversize has to fall in its present position. Such progress has been made since 1964 in the processes of reproduction in colour that it may be fairly claimed the beauty of the original plates has remained astonishingly constant. But, because botany and horticulture are expanding sciences, information about the plants has not. Therefore, faced with the alternatives of either printing a virtually useless facsimile of Curtis's text, or of correcting mistakes in the original and adding a plethora of footnotes to explain what would have been evident to eighteenth-century subscribers, or of rewriting the letterpress altogether incorporating the most recent available information, it seemed that the last would be less unsightly and more serviceable to the reader and certainly more in keeping with the declared intention of William Curtis who wished to interest and inform his subscribers about plants as well as share his own pleasure in their qualities.

T.W.

Acknowledgements

WE wish to acknowledge with thanks the kind co-operation and help of the Bentham-Moxon Trustees, present Proprietors and Publishers of the *Botanical Magazine*; the Director and Keeper of the Herbarium & Library and their staff at the Royal Botanic Gardens, Kew; the staff of the Botanic Garden and Institute of Systematic Botany of Zurich University; the staff of the Botanic Garden of the University of Bern; the Cambridge University Librarian and his assistants; the Librarian of the Linnean Society of London; the Reverend Alan Coldwells for his painstaking work upon this English edition; and Madame Ruth Schneebeli of Lucerne who first proposed that these beautiful plates deserved to be reissued.

T.W.   *C.C.*

Plant Names

THE urge to classify is a fundamental human instinct. In the early days of botany there were, unfortunately, no rules governing the system of classification and often the same plant carried many different names. At the relatively late date of 1753 Carl von Linné suggested a universally acceptable form of plant naming which is still used today. He chose a pair of Latin or latinized words for each plant species. In this book the identification of all the plants has been checked and all efforts made to give the correct botanic names. In some cases it was found that the plant illustrated in *Curtis's Botanical Magazine* was not correctly identified. For example, on Plate 100 the illustrated plant was called *Limnodorum tuberosum* but on checking was found to be another plant, *Calopogon pulchellus*. The name *Limnodorum tuberosum* appears in this book as a synonym and carries after the name 'sensu Bot. Mag.' which means it is the name used in the *Botanical Magazine*.

When the first volumes of *Curtis's Botanical Magazine* appeared botanists had little plant material available for their classification. It often happened that they had single isolated plant specimens. For example, they may have had solitary specimens from Greece, Italy, and Spain. It is likely that the three plants looked different, and each was given a different name. Today we have much more material to study and it is possible that these early 'species' are joined by masses of intermediate plants and what was earlier considered to be three separate species is today considered to be one species. This is more or less the case for the plant illustrated on Plate 1; the early species *Cistus villosus*, *C. polymorphus*, and *C. tauricus* are now considered to be no more than synonyms of *Cistus incanatus*.

Occasionally a plant was put in one genus and later transferred to another. For example, on Plate 13 the Winged Lotus was originally placed in the genus *Lotus*, later when botanists realized it was unlike other *Lotus* species it was transferred to the genus *Tetragonolobus*; the original name *Lotus tetragonolobus* appears as a synonym. In Europe there are on average about five synonyms for every species. In this book we have not attempted to list all synonyms but have included those that are frequently used in the literature. Introductions from outside Europe are often without synonyms and these form the majority in this selection.

The vernacular names cited in this book are those that in our opinion are more or less widely accepted but here we have had to select from masses of locally used names. On the whole, we have also rejected synthetic vernacular names derived from translations of the Latin because they rarely reflect our cultural inheritance. The information on the cultivation of the plants is given for a gardener in central or north-west Europe.

C.C.

Cistus incanus L.

HOARY, OR ROSE CISTUS, WHITE-LEAVED ROCK ROSE

FAMILY: Cistaceae
SYNONYMS: *Cistus villosus* sensu Bot. Mag., *C. polymorphus* Willk., *C. tauricus* C. Presl.
DISTRIBUTION: Mediterranean region
CULTIVATION: a species with many garden varieties and hybrids; not winter hardy, prefers well-drained, sandy soil, in full sun; propagated by softwood cuttings or by seed

THE Rock Roses that grow wild beside the Mediterranean and in the Near East have a strong claim to be amongst the oldest of all small flowering shrubs to be introduced into cultivation. Their flowers are not long-lasting. The petals open in the crinkly fashion of poppies but fall within eight hours. Yet they are so plentiful that a plant seems ablaze with colour, day after day, as long as there is sunshine. Moreover its sage-green leaves are the source of an aromatic gum called ladanum that for millennia has been used in medicine and as an ingredient of incense. In ancient Egypt bas-reliefs were carved showing Osiris carrying a scourge-like instrument believed by some scholars to be a ladanisterion, a rake with teeth of stiff leather used to thrash and bruise Cistus plants so that the sticky ladanum could afterwards be scraped from the thongs.

The Rock Rose was the precious myrrh, or *lôt*, of the Old Testament, though not the myrrh called *môr*, of the New. In Genesis Joseph was sold into slavery to a company of Ishmaelites *'with their camels bearing spices, and balm and myrrh'*. More than a thousand years afterwards the Greek historian Herodotus mentioned an easier, Arab way of collecting gum: from the beards of browsing goats who willynilly picked it up as they grazed the maquis. And, five hundred years after that, Dioscorides, the Greek physician to Antony and Cleopatra, included the plant in his catalogue of medical simples and made observations about processing the ladanum caught in goat beards.

The collection of the acrid brown gum must be amongst one of the most ancient of all trades as ladanum is still used in the manufacture of wound dressings and as a fixative in cheap cosmetics. Its scent is as readily recognisable as that of such pungent herbs as Mint and Thyme, Rosemary and Rue. To Napoleon it was always reminiscent of his native Corsica. To the expert in fragrances it comes closest, perhaps, to ambergris, that scented biliary secretion from the intestine of a spermaceti whale sometimes found floating in the oceans and seas.

Plate 1

Cistus incanus

Lilium candidum L.

WHITE LILY, ST. ANTHONY'S LILY, THE MADONNA LILY

FAMILY: Liliaceae
SYNONYM: *Lilium album* Houtt.
DISTRIBUTION: eastern Mediterranean region
CULTIVATION: hardy bulb; grows under a wide variety of conditions but prefers well-drained, humus-rich soil in a fairly sunny position; propagated by bulb offsets or by seed

THE White Lily is figured on Cretan vases and frescoes that are nearly four thousand years old, and for an untraceable length of time it has been grown as a vegetable in the East, the Japanese especially relishing the bulb served with a sweet white sauce. Wild colonies have been found in the West but most colonies were once domesticated within an area which roughly corresponds with the size of the Roman Empire at its largest extent in AD 117. This indicates it was spread by the legionaries for they highly regarded the plant's properties to heal wounds and soothe corns. Since it has been credited with other properties, to cure epilepsy and dropsy, as a treatment for baldness, or to '*trimly deck a blank place with hair*', and Curtis noted '*we are gravely told that it taketh away the wrinkles of the face*'. He was truly eighteenth century in his cynicism, yet, looked at in another way, few flowers are so lovely or more capable of temporarily easing lines of care.

Virgil had named the species *candidum* because it was of such a rich, glistening white, and in Imperial Rome Lilies shared the status of the Rose, measurably half a category above the esteem enjoyed by the Violet, the Anemone, the Narcissus, and the Hyacinth. Because they decorated every banquet and were required throughout the year, Lilies were grown by the Romans' Syrian gardeners in forcing houses glazed with gypsum and heated by hot-water pipes.

The advanced skills of Roman horticulture were lost in the Dark Ages, but the Emperor Charlemagne put the White Lily first on the list of the plants ordered for his garden, and the Church, which kept Western civilization alive, associated the Lily with two saints: the Blessed Virgin and St. Anthony of Padua. We see them in paintings and sculptures carrying a Lily like a sceptre, and so the plant became known as St. Anthony's or the Madonna Lily.

Unlike most species of the genus, White Lilies give two distinct performances. First, in high summer, comes the spectacular flowering when the stems, with small leaf stems attached, race up to 1.5 metres (5 feet) or more. After a rich month the dead head is cut, and later, the brittle stalk is tugged from the bulb and the hole plugged with sand to prevent the entry of pests. There follows the second performance in autumn. A tussock of basal leaves surges upwards like a fountain. The leaves are lettuce-green and slightly undulated. From a distance they resemble huge rosettes of Hart's-tongue Ferns or, what they are to a discerning Japanese, a most exotic vegetable.

Plate 2

Lilium candidum

Ornithogalum nutans L.

NEOPOLITAN, OR DROOPING STAR OF BETHLEHEM

FAMILY: Liliaceae
DISTRIBUTION: southern and eastern Europe, Asia Minor, naturalized elsewhere
CULTIVATION: hardy bulb; propagated by bulb offsets or by seeds

A NUMBER of species of *Ornithogalum* are edible; the unopened shoots of a Balkan species being eaten like Asparagus, and the bulbs of *O. nutans* and *O. umbellatum* being long cultivated as a source of food round the eastern Mediterranean. Jewish history gives an indication of how long. In about 890 BC, when Ben-hadad, King of Syria, invested the Israelites in Samaria, the besieged were reduced to cannibalism, donkeys' heads and doves' dung. But in fact the Jews were not forced to eat pigeon guano. Doves' Dung was the common name for both *O. nutans* and *O. umbellatum* and was not inappropriate. A mass of their flowers does have the white, dotted appearance of bird droppings. Dioscorides noted the same characteristic. In his list of plants he named them from two Greek words: *ornis* (bird) and *gala* (milk). The Arabs have a name equivalent to Doves' Dung as a comprehensive term for a number of vegetables, but they most commonly use it for *Ornithogalum*. The plants are still familiar to Muslim pilgrims because a flour manufactured from the dried bulbs is part of their diet en route to Mecca.

The curious and long English name given in the *Botanical Magazine* is a literal translation of the name chosen by the Fleming, Charles de L'Ecluse, a Renaissance scholar whose name was Latinized to Clusius. Though well born and endowed with a great intellect, Clusius had a wretched life. In the 17th century religious wars his father's estate was sequestered, his uncle was executed, and he himself so impoverished that he had no real security until he was an old man and the Dutch offered him a chair at their new university of Leyden. Clusius's consolations were scholarly and he was very highly regarded as a botanist. As a young man he hunted plants in Iberia, and all through his life he was sent dried plants and seeds and other vegetative parts from all over the Western world. One specimen was a Doves' Dung bulb which, simply because it arrived in a consignment from Naples, he named *O. neapolitanum*.

More than a hundred years afterwards Linnaeus altered the name in case there should be any misunderstanding about the plant's provenance. He called it *O. nutans* because the white and jade flowers hung downwards. But even this was not entirely satisfactory. Some say there are two varieties, one shorter and indigenous to southern Europe. The taller eastern plant they name *O.n.* var. *boucheanum*. Botanists call such meticulous namers 'splitters'. The rest, content with only two, are called 'lumpers'.

Plate 3

Ornithogalum nutans

Alcea rosea L.

HOLLYHOCK

FAMILY: Malvaceae
SYNONYMS: *Althaea flexuosa* Sims
DISTRIBUTION: origin uncertain, south-east Europe, Asia Minor, Persia and India
CULTIVATION: hardy perennial, or some races biennial or annual; prefers well-drained soil and a sunny position; propagated by seed or choice varieties may be divided by stem cuttings or the whip method of grafting. There are many garden varieties and some hybrids with *Alcea filifolia* L.; they are rather less popular today because of their susceptibility to rust disease.

No one knows when the Hollyhock was first introduced into cultivation but the species from the Near East was mentioned as a common English garden flower in a manuscript of about 1440 which establishes its old age. The seeds of *A. rosea* were said to have been brought from China in 1573 to invigorate and enrich the existing European stock.

Charles I's botanist, John Parkinson, who in 1629 published the first gardening dictionary in English with a pun in his title, *Paradisi in sole Paradisus terrestris* – the terrestrial park of Park-in-sun – described a number of 'Holliock' varieties. There were singles and doubles, and of many colours, one '*a dark red like black bloud*'.

Hollyhocks have never lacked popularity and in the 19th century they won the accolade of being florists' flowers. Florists then had no connection with those who bought and sold cut flowers and pot plants. They were a noble race of men, chiefly artisans, who spent their fortunes and all their leisure in improving certain chosen flowers. Much of their patient work on the Hollyhock was lost to us because in 1866 rust disease began to infect the plants and they were almost wiped out. It was noted that Hollyhocks in the areas of heavy industry were more resistant than others, presumably because the rust parasites could not stand the toxic-laden air. Attempts to breed tough perennial strains from these Hollyhocks and the vigorous Fig Leaf species, *A. ficifolia*, were only partially successful and so today the plants are grown as annuals or, more usually, as biennials, a few seeds being planted each year for continuity. This has lessened but not eliminated the danger of rust. An attack of the disease is easily diagnosed: hideous orange blotches deface the upperside of the leaves; red pimples break out on the underside. These have to be burnt immediately and the plant dusted with sulphur every third day. At the end of the season, should there be anything left to bother about, the top growth must be destroyed by fire. Despite this particular danger *A. rosea* is well worth growing. It has a special attractiveness exactly caught by the artist and engraver of the plate. In its native China it is also grown as an economic plant, the fibres of the stem being used like hemp, the dried petals as the source of a blue-black dye, the leaves as a pot-herb, the boiled roots as a popular remedy for chestiness, and the flowers prized as vegetables.

Plate 4

Alcea rosea

Syringa vulgaris L.

COMMON LILAC

FAMILY: Oleaceae
DISTRIBUTION: Europe: in the Balkans, naturalized elsewhere
CULTIVATION: hardy shrub; prefers sunny position and loamy soil; propagated by cuttings or by layers

MANY scientific names have 'L.' or 'Linn.' placed after them to credit Linnaeus as their namer. It pays tribute to his standing as a naturalist. Born a hundred years after the unhappy Clusius, Linnaeus lived much the same sort of life though with more ample fortune. As a young man he made two botanical explorations, travelled about Europe, spent a brief period practising as a physician, and then devoted himself exclusively to natural history at Uppsala university. Undisturbed by other passions, for his marriage was unsatisfactory and he enjoyed only what he called 'botanical romances', he had the leisure to earn the respect of the learned world and the title of 'The Great Systematist'. It was he who named Lilac *Syringa* because it had tubular flowers and *syrinx* was the Greek for tube. Unaware of this, a contemporary botanist used the same name for what the English know as Mock Orange and which Linnaeus had earlier called *Philadelphus*. There is a rule, tiresome to many but of value to botanists, that unless there is a good scientific reason for a change the first name is given priority. In both these cases Linnaeus had priority and his names stand, though *Syringa* still means Lilac to some gardeners and Mock Orange to others.

Syringa vulgaris, introduced from Eastern Europe long before the 16th century, has become so common that in abandoned places it can be a pest and birds carry its seeds into hedge bottoms. Before it was seized on by breeders Lilac gave its name to a particular colour in many languages although plants raised from seed were always inclined to vary in shade. Perhaps this accounts for the slight distinction shown in the plate. Undoubtedly garden hybrids have developed spontaneously that are basically lilac-coloured but are also touched with blue or violet or purple or deep rose. These are the closest relations to the *Syringa vulgaris* of Linnaeus though in most gardens they have been replaced by half a hundred and more cultivars bred from carefully selected parents.

Lilac is also in great demand as a cut flower. Two-year-old plants with up to a dozen shoots have their roots sliced so that they can be thrust into small pots. Their food, water, light, and air supplies are rigidly controlled, and their blooming held back by refrigeration or advanced by warm baths or etherization. The process seems to have much in common with the intense farming of animals and poultry, and the end product is rarely to the liking of true connoisseurs of Lilac.

Plate 5

Syringa vulgaris

Jasminum officinale L.

JESSAMINE, COMMON JASMINE, POET'S JESSAMINE

FAMILY: Oleaceae
DISTRIBUTION: Persia, North India, China, naturalized elsewhere
CULTIVATION: hardy self-supporting climber; prefers well-drained soil; propagated by cuttings

THE Jessamine or Common Jasmine reached Europe travelling along the Eastern trade routes from China and North India and Persia in the first half of the 16th century. It evidently had a medical value as the specific name, *officinale*, tells us it was used as a simple in an apothecary's shop. Its fruit is poisonous but herbals recommended the flowers as a sedative and a syrup from them for treating throat complaints. Jasmine's chief value, however, has always lain in its scent, and not only as a scent in itself but also as the prime foundation of the most expensive and beautiful of all blends. Successful blending was always a commercial secret, but because Jasmine was so ubiquitous anyone could try his hand at it, and many did. It is noteworthy that in 1770 an enlightened British Parliament introduced legislation to protect His Majesty's subjects from being tricked into matrimony by 'scents, paints, cosmetics, washes, artificial teeth, false hair, Spanish wool, iron stays, high-heeled shoes, and bolstered hips'. Conviction automatically annulled the marriage.

In southern Europe and especially in the Alpes-Maritimes Jasmine-growing became so profitable that, like the farmers of ancient Rome who tore out their Olives to make room for the flowers required for banquets, the peasants took to cultivating Jasmine rather than barley on their terraces. They still do, though now, to save providing supports, *J. officinale* is used as a parent for grafting-in scions of *J. grandiflorum*, a native of the Himalaya. These make stout bushes about a metre (3 feet) high with larger and more profuse flowers and thus the essential scent is preserved and multiplied in quantity. An extraordinary fact is that, in the process of *enfleurage*, or extracting the scent by absorbing flowers in an oil, the actual amount contained in the flower is replaced by oil which itself then becomes scent. The total amount is therefore far, far greater than the first minute drop.

For centuries the climbing Jasmine has been grown over arbours and summer houses and bowers and has been closely associated with romance. It is a fancy to speculate how often its tiny flowers have been used in posies and bridal bouquets, how often they have been dried and pressed as keepsakes.

16

Plate 6

Jasminum officinale

Origanum dictamnus L.

DITTANY OF CRETE

FAMILY: Labiatae
SYNONYMS: *Amaracus dictamnus* (L.) Bentham, *A. tomentosus* Moench
DISTRIBUTION: Crete
CULTIVATION: tender sub-shrub; prefers dry, clay soil, must be kept relatively dry in winter; propagated by cuttings or seed

THE genus *Origanum* has about twenty-five species which have been variously used for medicine and seasoning, as strewing herbs and for rubbing on furniture, as the source of a brown dye and, before the general use of hops in brewing, *O. vulgare* was much in demand for making ale. One of the most attractive of all the species is the Dittany of Crete. Its small marked leaves are downy and the flowers droop in spikelets, and it has charmed generations of country people who grew it in their windows, calling it the Hop Plant.

It was first written up by William Turner, twice deprived Dean of Wells in Somerset, and one of the first in the long line of clergymen of all nationalities who have so well served natural history. But this is not to say Turner was likeable. On the contrary, he was a most objectionable parson; bigoted, self-opinionated, litigatious, and coarse-mannered. The abrupt changes of religion in his day thrust him to an eminence in the English Church he would never have reached under ordinary circumstances, and it is notable that even when he was installed as Dean of Wells for the second time he was so disputatious that he had to be suspended from office. It gives no pleasure to English botanists to accept such a clerical boor as the founding father of their science, but, though he had the failings of credulity common to contemporary herbalists, Turner's *Herbal* of 1568 did mark the beginning of botany in England and demonstrated his skill for noting relevancies which even a highly trained botanist of this century might miss. He noticed, for instance, that the stamens of the White Lily had a different scent from that of the rest of the flower.

Turner noted of the Dittany that, mixed with barley meal, it made a good purge. *'The roote hath an hoote taste, it speedeth the deliverance of children.'* These are provable facts. Unfortunately, he then takes us from the world of science to that of fable by asserting: *'The juice dronke with wine is a remedy against the bitings of serpentes'*. This particular virtue is attributed haphazardly to so many medicinal plants by so many herbalists that it would seem that venomous creatures played a considerable part in their lives. Dittany at any rate could offer a last consolation. It was the belief of the Cretans and Greeks that if the plant thrived on a grave it showed the corpse below was both joyful and at peace.

Plate 7

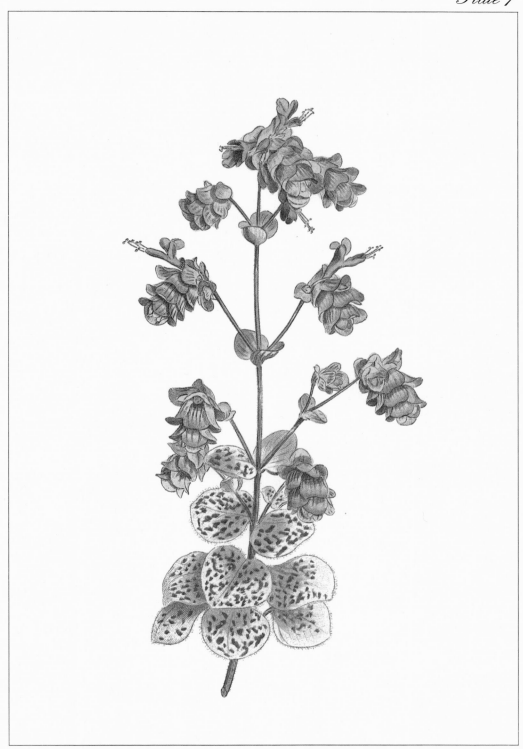

Origanum dictamnus

Tulipa suaveolens Roth

EARLY DWARF TULIP

FAMILY: Liliaceae
DISTRIBUTION: origin uncertain and disputed – almost certainly not South Russia as usually cited, perhaps Asia Minor. This species is probably an ancestor of the cultivated tulip or perhaps it is one of the very early cultivated tulips
CULTIVATION: hardy bulb; propagated by bulb offsets or by seed

Like Linnaeus after him, Konrad von Gessner was a scholar who married the wrong woman and consoled himself with hard work. He was a Zuricher and lived from 1516 to 1565, lectured in letters, natural philosophy and Greek, and received many honours. Known as 'the German Pliny' he absorbed and exuded knowledge, publishing books on a variety of subjects from plants to mountain climbing. He made a point of climbing at least one mountain every year for the exercise and the plants he found on the way.

Before 1559 the Emperor's ambassador to Suleiman the Magnificent introduced Tulips to Europe. Gessner saw them growing for the first time in Augsburg and published a description of them with a plate. Probably they were *T. suaveolens* figured here. Nevertheless, as he was the first to describe the plant, Gessner's name was loosely used for all Tulips introduced from the Ottoman Empire at that period. *T. gessneriana* was therefore the parent of all 'garden Tulips' as opposed to wild species; and escapes of *T. gessneriana* which have naturalized and then been 'discovered' are put under the single title of *Neo-tulipae*.

The unfortunate Clusius now enters the Tulip story. Tulips had been sent to him by other botanists and, at the time of his move to Leyden, his collection was the only thing of value he possessed. Scarcely had he settled in than he was robbed of the lot. The stolen goods were used to stock the seventeen provinces of the Netherlands and Clusius farcically described as founder of the Dutch bulb-growing industry.

Tulip-growing soon became a passion and bulbs were an important article of commerce. There was a trade in 'paper Tulips' that did not yet exist but were promised. The price of real bulbs ballooned. A law was introduced to regulate the maximum price of a single bulb to £400. It was ignored. The whole thing was as lunatic and unsafe as the South Sea Bubble. It burst in the same way. Thousands were ruined as confidence in the Tulip standard waned.

As if one craze was not enough, a second began a hundred years afterwards in Turkey, the native land of many Tulip species. The Sultan and his subjects gave Tulip parties round their kiosks; the guests eating luxuries, drinking sherbert, listening to music, and above all admiring the beds of Tulips illuminated by lanterns carried through the pleasure grounds attached to the backs of crawling tortoises.

Plate 8

Tulipa suaveolens

Clematis integrifolia L.

ENTIRE-LEAVED CLEMATIS, VIRGIN'S BOWER

FAMILY: Ranunculaceae
DISTRIBUTION: south-east Europe, Near East
CULTIVATION: hardy, somewhat woody perennial; prefers damp soil; propagated by dividing the rootstock

A SPECIES of Clematis that does not climb is unusual. *Clematis integrifolia* has no generally accepted common name and is one of the few. It is a perennial which grows to a metre (3 feet) in height with a stem that is generally soft but can become woody. The plant has two attractions. One, shown clearly in the plate, is the perfect balance of its structure. The elliptical leaves, wider where they join the stem than at their point, are arranged in pairs opposite to one another and from the axils spring stems with leaflets. Its other attraction, not evident from the plate, is the curious construction of the cream and indigo inflorescence. It has no petals. The four, veined, petal-like objects are sepals. Nor does it secrete honey. The colour is not constant, and varies from shades of purple through blue to white.

C. integrifolia was a late 16th century introduction into cultivation and its provenance has been variously attributed to Germany, Hungary, and southern Europe. The first to describe it was the Swiss, Kaspar Bauhin, who lived from 1560 to 1624, anticipated Linnaeus's binomary system and adopted his own orderly methods of diagnosing the characteristics of plants. He has been called 'last of the classical botanists'. Doubtless he would have preferred the title 'first of the systematists'. His position in botany is unique in that he was the first to write up a local flora, the flora of his native city Basel, though like all other early floras it also included garden plants, vegetables, and agricultural crops. His great work, the *Pinax*, was the result of years of study and correspondence with herbalists and botanists who lived far beyond that area of Europe where modern botany originated. He even received records from places as far distant and, at that time, primitive as Scotland. In 1623 he published his assembled material, and the *Pinax* recorded all the species of plants known to him. It included *C. integrifolia* which he called *Clematitis* and described as blue-flowered and upstanding.

The next to write up the plant was John Parkinson in his *Paradisi* of 1629. He changed the spelling to 'Clematis', agreed with the colour, and added an English name, 'The Hungarian Climber'. As the species belongs to the non-climbers this was rather peculiar. A hundred years after that Linnaeus gave the plant its accepted botanic name and noted that it was the one species in the genus with single straight-edged, egg- to lance-shaped leaves. He added that it had nodding flowers.

Plate 9

Clematis integrifolia

Fritillaria imperialis L.

CROWN IMPERIAL

FAMILY: Liliaceae
DISTRIBUTION: western Himalaya and Persia, naturalized elsewhere
CULTIVATION: hardy bulbous plant; prefers heavy undisturbed soil; propagated by bulb offsets or by seed

THE Crown Imperial is a bold, dramatic plant. The bulbs are the size of a man's clenched fist and have a dent in the top. Planted in the usual way there is a danger of water settling in the dent and starting rot. Therefore they should be planted on their sides and, once covered, they ought to be left alone to settle and multiply. They resent disturbance. Then, though tall and magnificent as the plate makes clear, they stink like a fox's earth. For these reasons alone they require careful siting in a garden. There are natural yellow varieties as well as bronze red, and one, *F.i. inodora*, a native of Bokhara, lacks that foxy smell.

The first Crown Imperial came from Turkey to Vienna in 1576, having travelled from its original home in the western Himalaya along the ancient trade route through Kabul, Herat, Nishapur, Tabriz, and Trebizond. Allegedly the bulbs were cooked and eaten in Persia. It is unlikely that any sort of cooking would have rendered them harmless or even palatable. They are acrid and contain a colourless alkaloid now named imperialine which is a heart poison. Even honey made from the nectar is said to be emetic to those who have delicate digestions.

Clusius received the plant in the Imperial gardens, named it *Lilium persicum*, and gradually it was distributed throughout Europe. Being so decorative it found its way into the flower paintings of a number of the Dutch old masters. It was greeted by botanists as a curiosity both on account of the whorl of leaves sprouting like a tuft of hair above the flowers, and because the large nectaries at the base of the petals contained a drop of nectar which, if shaken out, was immediately replaced. It was just the sort of plant to excite imaginations. A legend sprang up, of which there are at least three variants in detail, that it alone amongst all flowers stared boldly at Our Lord on his way to Calvary and, ever since, has hung its petals in shame, its nectaries filled with tears.

Parkinson declared the plant's '*stately beautifulness gives it the first place in his garden of delight*' and named it 'The Crowne Imperiall' which was translated into many European languages. Linnaeus tidied up the botanic name. The plant belonged to the general Lily family but was a Fritillary. He added Parkinson's splendid name as the specific.

Plate 10

Fritillaria imperialis

Argemone mexicana L.

PRICKLY POPPY, DEVIL'S FIG, MEXICAN ARGEMONE, MEXICAN POPPY

FAMILY: Papaveraceae
DISTRIBUTION: warmer parts of America, now naturalized in Europe, Africa, Asia, and Australia
CULTIVATION: usually cultivated as summer annual but some races are biennial or perennial; prefers well-drained, sunny places

THE Devil's Fig was introduced to Europe from the Americas before the last decade of the sixteenth century. It was written up by Clusius who decided it was a Poppy and especially commended its prickly, silver-blotched foliage and lustrous, oddly scented flowers that varied in shade from orange to yellow.

Botanists examining the plant's structure fell into two groups; one, following Clusius, called it *Papaver*; others, considering it a Thistle, called it *Carduus*. Then Linnaeus put his mind to the matter. He accepted that it belonged to the Poppy family but saw slight dissimilarities, principally in the fruit capsules, and he proposed a new name entirely, choosing *Argemone* as *argema* was the Greek for cataract and the plant's gamboge-yellow sap was reputed to soothe cataractous eyes. He gave it the specific name *mexicana* either because it was first found there or because it was so common a weed in that region. In fact, as his correspondents and their published works made clear, the plant's provenance was widespread through the American tropics. The West Indies claimed it. So did Peru. And from rather an unlikely source, a book on insects, botanists were made aware it also grew in Surinam.

The book was published in 1705, the work of an intrepid Dutch lady who was precursor of many other intrepid ladies who have gone all over the world to sketch natural history subjects. Maria Sibylla Merian's achievement was remarkable when we recall how few people travelled about Europe unattended in the late sixteenth century, and that she took two long, uncomfortable, and dangerous sea voyages, accompanied only by her daughter and their servants, in an era when the death-rate on ships to the Indies was extremely high. Furthermore, Surinam was largely unexplored territory, had a disagreeable climate, and some of the subjects of her brush and pencil were both loathsome and deadly. That she survived was something of a miracle. So was her folio of engraved and coloured plates, one of the most splendid books ever published, which showed for the first time the pineapple, the cassava, the castor-oil plant, the guava, and the pawpaw, and a great many others besides. Amongst them, showing how widely it was spread throughout the tropics of America, was a plate of *A. mexicana*, its prickly leaves the host of a winged beetle, a pair of evil-looking insects, and two fine grubs.

Plate 11

Argemone mexicana

Hermodactylus tuberosus (L.) Miller

SNAKE'S-HEAD, WIDOW IRIS

FAMILY: Iridaceae

SYNONYM: *Iris tuberosa* L.

DISTRIBUTION: central and eastern Mediterranean region, naturalized elsewhere

CULTIVATION: generally hardy but does not withstand extreme frosts; needs a well-drained place and prefers a sunny position; propagated by division of the rootstock

IT is a convention that if the date of the introduction of a plant is not known or cannot be properly estimated, it may be counted from the date of publication of a work describing or merely listing it as a cultivated plant. Therefore all early botanists' stirpium and floras, gardeners' lists, and herbals have an historic as well as a scientific interest. One gardener, whose name featured often in the *Botanical Magazine*, was John Gerard, an English surgeon-barber who in 1596 issued a list of the plants he himself was growing as well as the *Herball* in 1597 that brought him fame. He was a plagiarist, lifting almost all the plates and information about plants from contemporaries without making any acknowledgement or payment, and he was the sort of cheat who plants a specimen by night to 'discover' it next day. Nevertheless he dearly loved plants and had an expressive prose style. The plate of the Snake's-Head and the succeeding ten plates in this volume are all given 1596 as the date of their introduction because Gerard was cultivating them at that time.

Gerard's name for this plant was Velvet Flower-de-Luce. The fleur-de-lis, so frequently found in heraldry, was a medieval misnomer. The emblem of the French kings was an Iris, not a Lily. Gerard probably knew this, but evidently he was unaware that Snake's-Head was not an Iris. Botanical dissection shows that an Iris has ovaries with three cells and the Snake's-Head an ovary with only one. There is only this slight difference but it exists and therefore they are put in separate genera.

In translation *Hermodactylus* means 'the finger of Hermes', and though it is difficult to see any connection with Hermes, the tuberous bulb might be said to resemble a crooked little finger. A legend had been dug up that oriental ladies once used the powdered root as a rouge cosmetic which suggests it was in cultivation long before Gerard grew it in London. But there is no evidence and we abide by the convention. Small, fragile, slightly fragrant, and sombre, it is regarded as weird by some plantsmen but it has very many admirers. Gerard graphically described its exquisite colouring as '*blackness welted about with a goose-turd green*'.

Plate 12

Hermodactylus tuberosus

Tetragonolobus purpureus Moench

WINGED LOTUS

FAMILY: Leguminosae
SYNONYM: *Lotus tetragonolobus* L.
DISTRIBUTION: southern Europe to lat. 47° N. in the Ukraine, and Mediterranean region
CULTIVATION: non-hardy annual; prefers well-drained, sunny places

WILD peas have never been favourably regarded as free food because some have a sharp flavour. However, in 1555 when John Gerard was a boy of 10 living in the north country town of Nantwich, there was so great a famine that the starving English scoured shores and woods and hedge bottoms for Sea Peas and all kinds of Vetches to keep themselves alive. It was not the sort of disaster Gerard would be likely to forget, yet, when he was growing Mediterranean Winged Lotus or Bird's-foot Trefoil in 1596, he made no mention that it was edible. Nor did any of his contemporaries. One of them did note that the seeds were exported by the Italians but he omitted to say for what purpose. This was singular. The plant was recommended as an annual that should be allowed to run prostrate or tumble over banks or walls or be grown up structures of peasticks, and was highly regarded by gardeners. Parkinson wrote it up, calling it long-windedly 'the Crimson-blossomed or Square-codded Pease'. Only Philip Miller, in charge of the Apothecaries' Garden in London, noted 138 years after Gerard had produced his list that in former times the Lotus's quaint pods had been dressed and eaten. No one troubled to remark on the fact that it was an esculent much sought after by epicures and called the *Asparagus Pea*. The pods were harvested when young and tender and no longer than a thumbnail, regularly picked to ensure a long cropping period, and they were steamed or boiled for a very short time and eaten whole. They still are by a knowing few, the eaters and appreciators of such esoteric vegetables as Hyacinth Beans, Black Spanish Radishes, Roka, and Good King Henry. The export of ripe seeds by Italians is explained by the fact that for a long time they were used as an inexpensive substitute for coffee beans.

The Asparagus Pea has a new role today. Epicures continue to cultivate it as a table vegetable, but in the sunny Mediterranean countries where the plants are native, the little pods are rarely seen in the street markets. Now, being tolerant of aridity, Asparagus Peas are sometimes grown as a forage plant, and either fed fresh after wilting to beasts in the stall, or made into nutritious silage.

Plate 13

Tetragonolobus purpureus

Helleborus Niger L.

CHRISTMAS ROSE, BLACK HELLEBORE

FAMILY: Ranunculaceae
DISTRIBUTION: central and southern Europe, and West Asia
CULTIVATION: hardy perennial; prefers well-drained, calcareous soil and partial shade;
propagated by dividing the rootstock

IN wintertime many of the wooded uplands in Europe are enriched by evergreen Hellebores that stand out vividly against the leafless undergrowth. They are outstanding foliage plants, having shining, deeply cut, heavy leaves; and their flowers have a sculptured quality and vary in colour from plum purple through a mixture of cream and rust, tawny yellow and willow green to the lightest coloured of all, the Christmas Rose. The blackness of the root explains why the species is named *H. niger*. The white corolla of petals is sometimes blushed or freckled with rose and gradually the petals turn green. When they are the colour of the leaves it is a sign the plant has been fertilized.

The plate indicates a certain solidity and toughness, and it is surprising how much cold the plant can resist, but sleet and rain can bruise and brown the flowers so careful gardeners protect them under hand-glasses. They have attracted the attention of the flower trade and the practitioners of forcing make sure there are plenty of supplies at Christmas. Alone of the Hellebores they can tolerate warm rooms, but if they are to last, they should be put in a cool, moist place at night time. In a bland climate, growing out of doors, they are true to their name, especially if the preceding summer has been hot, and they flower steadily from Christmas, sometimes for several weeks.

Pliny the Elder, the Admiral killed in the eruption of Vesuvius in AD 79, was a distinguished Roman naturalist who noted the Black Hellebore in his *Naturalis Historia*. The plant would have reminded him of his native province Como, where to this day Christmas Roses grow in profusion. He mentioned the plant's root as a purgative and cure for lunacy. So did Gerard who said that *'Hellebor is good for mad and furious men'*. It must have been a desperate remedy for desperate cases because the pitch-coloured root contains two poisons. Undoubtedly the root's primary use in more credulous times was connected with sorcery. Traditionally, even collecting it was dangerous. It had to be done in a certain way; first drawing a circle round the plant with steel, and saying prescribed spells as the root was lifted. It was also important that an eagle should not witness the process or the gatherer would soon waste and die.

Plate 14

Helleborus niger

Lamium orvala L.

BALM-LEAVED ARCHANGEL, DEADNETTLE, DRAGON FLOWER

FAMILY: Labiatae

DISTRIBUTION: Europe: from northern Italy and western Austria to western Yugoslavia

CULTIVATION: hardy perennial; prefers well-drained, humus-rich soil in shade; usually propagated by seed but can be divided by cuttings

THE Lamiums, with about a hundred other genera, are native to the colossal Eurasian continental mass north of the tropics from the North Atlantic to the North Pacific. Pliny gave them their name, mentioning Lamium four times in his long work on natural history, and we translate it as Deadnettle, a word which to the majority of people immediately evokes the idea of an invasive garden pest. Therefore we must apply the definition of a weed as a plant in the wrong place, and this is not true of many of the Deadnettles. It is particularly untrue of the plant called *Lamium orvala*, or sometimes *Orvala lamioides*, which grows wild in parts of Europe and has collected an assortment of English names; Balm-leaved Archangel, Hungary Deadnettle, and Dragon Flower. Like many supposed weeds the Dragon Flower can add much to a flower garden if it is well treated and fed; and, grown as a single specimen in a 30-centimetre (12-inch) pot in a cool greenhouse, it will reach a height of 1.5 metres (5 feet), need staking, and have abundant, large-sized flowers of coral red and purple.

The Dragon Flower is an excellent subject to demonstrate the truth there are many ways of looking at a plant. The gardener sees it as a weed or an attractive perennial or even a petted exotic. The botanist is able to reduce his picture of the Deadnettle to a simple vertical section, a floral diagram, and a formula: $†♀\overline{K}(5)C(5)A2+2\underline{G}(2)$. To the majority of people who care for plants this attractive and almost entirely accurate plate is quite sufficient. But there are those lovers of the quaint and curious who wish to know more; that as the flower petals are virtually united and look like a pair of lips, the top lip hooded and the lower with a drooping appendage, the plant belongs to the *Labiatae* family because the Latin *labiatus* means lipped. Most of all they will delight in discovering something that is quite unobservable in the plate, the beauty of the stamens lying side by side. To see this a plant has to be plucked and examined upside down. Finally, there are those whose primary interest is utilitarian, and they appreciate that the Dragon Flower is attractive to bees; good fodder for horses, sheep, and goats, though cows will not touch it; a tolerable spinach substitute in the kitchen; and boiled and fed with meal to hounds it makes a bracing tonic after a winter's hunting.

Plate 15

Lamium orvala

Anemone coronaria L.

POPPY, OR ST. BRIGID ANEMONE

FAMILY: Ranunculaceae
DISTRIBUTION: Mediterranean region, Asia Minor, and Persia
CULTIVATION: a tuberous perennial that does not withstand severe frosts; prefers well-drained but not dry garden loam with plenty of well-rotted manure, likes some shade; propagated by tuber offsets or seed, the tubers are usually lifted in summer. It is often grown or forced in frames or greenhouses for cut flowers in winter or spring. It is very variable in nature and there are many garden varieties and hybrids with *Anemone hortensis*, *A. pavonina*, and *A. hortensis* × *A. pavonina*

THE claim that Shen Nung, the 'Divine Cultivator', was the first to produce a treatise on plants in about 2700 BC is scarcely valid in view of the fact that in his day there was no written language. Therefore the honour partly falls to Aristotle whose botanical works were lost and partly to his pupil Theophrastus who wrote down what he remembered of the originals and added observations of his own in the 4th century BC. It was Theophrastus who named the Anemone after *anemos*, the Greek for wind, as the downy fruits are dispersed by wind, and the name tenaciously survived despite the fact that his *Enquiry into Plants* went through the mincing machine of multi-translation being turned from Greek into Syrian, then into Arabic, and then into Latin before being put back into Greek again. Gerard was the first to list it in 1596 as being in cultivation, though it may well have been long before. As the name *coronaria* implies, the plant was popularly used for garlands in antiquity, and called by the Greeks 'Blood of Adonis'. The early Christians, with their sensible adaptability, promptly renamed it 'Blood Drops of Christ'. At the time of the Second Crusade earth ballast brought in ships from Palestine was dumped in the Pisa burial ground and the Anemones that sprang up were said to symbolize the blood of Christian martyrs. Legends accrue to such plants. There is a persisting tale that a Parisian developed a certain strain of Anemone so prized that seeds were only got from him by the sleight of hand of a burgomaster of Antwerp. This is why in North America varieties of the species are still called French Anemones.

Both in the wild and in gardens the spectrum of colours is wide. Gerard noted, '*Myselfe have in my garden twelve different sorts*'. Parkinson was exuberant about '*Windeflowers so full of variety and so dainty*', and he made a useful note of their indifference to '*the smoake of brewers, dyers, or mault-kilns*'. By the eighteenth century *A. coronaria* had become a florists' flower, and still more varieties were bred. Perfection was aimed for in the colour of the band and the tracery of veins in the flowers and in the clear sea-green of the ferny leaves. And a special Anemone compost was made up, composed of less exotic and revolting ingredients than was customary amongst the florists: simply two parts of well-rotted hazel leaf mould to one part of mature cow dung; the heap turned occasionally to ensure even mellowing and mixing; and kept for no less than a year.

Plate 16

Anemone coronaria

Hibiscus trionum L.

BLADDER HIBISCUS, KETMIA, GOODNIGHT-AT-NOON, FLOWER-OF-AN-HOUR

FAMILY: Malvaceae
SYNONYMS: *Hibiscus africans* Mill. H., *H. vesicarius* Cav.
DISTRIBUTION: warmer parts of the Old World
CULTIVATION: usually cultivated as a half-hardy annual but it is perennial in a heated greenhouse; propagated by seed

GERARD noted that the plants of goodnight-at-noon which prospered in his garden in 1596 were '*transplanted from the African Woods*'. Wherever it sprang from originally its present distribution covers a much larger stretch of territory known to botanists as the Old World Tropics which ranges from South Africa to the Pacific Islands. Being an annual and a free seeder, self-sown plants grow in large numbers each year, and this might account for it being so widespread. Experts are at one in recommending it for easy culture in a well-sheltered place. Left undisturbed it will colonize a part of the garden, growing annually on hairy stems from 60 to 100 centimetres (2 to 3 feet), with prettily lobed leaves and flowers as broad as a pocket watch. Its flower parts are arranged in sets of five: there are five petals; the calyx has five teeth; there are five styles; the stamens are united in a five-sided column; and the fruit capsule has five valves which, when dry, open to act like a pepperpot and liberally scatter ripe seeds in the neighbourhood. It is tougher than most half-hardy annuals but responds best of all to being treated as a pot plant in a greenhouse.

Goodnight-at-noon is a descriptive name because the flowers generally open in the forenoon for about an hour. For the same reason it has also been called Flower-of-an-hour. However, strains have developed, by the agencies of chance and man, which are considerably less coy and they will flower all day. Amongst its other common names is Bladder Hibiscus, presumably because the calyx blows up as it matures. It has showy cousins like the vermilion Chinese Shoeflower and the Jamaica Sorrel, and it is also related to an edible Hibiscus, much used in oriental cooking and in soups, called elegantly Ladies' Fingers and most inelegantly Gumbo.

Plate 17

Hibiscus trionum

Muscari comosum (L.) Miller

TASSEL HYACINTH

FAMILY: Liliaceae
SYNONYMS: *Hyacinthus comosus* L., *Leopoldia comosum* (L.) Parl.
DISTRIBUTION: southern and central Europe, Near East, North Africa, naturalized
northern and western Europe
CULTIVATION: hardy bulb; propagated by bulb offsets or by seed

AN Anglo-Saxon, translating and annotating the list of medical herbs compiled by Dioscorides, gave the Grape Hyacinth a most sinister provenance: '*It is said it was produced out of dragon's blood, on the tops of mountains, in thick forests.*' In fact, it is a native all round the Mediterranean, being an invader of olive groves.

The peculiar arrangement of the urn-shaped flowers of *M. comosum* is interesting botanically. The dense cluster of flowers at the top of the spike is attractive, but the flowers are sterile. Those that matter, the ones which attract insects and are fertile, are the rather less interesting, spread-out, green and amethyst flowers below.

In the 16th century many species were grown, Gerard listing *M. comosum* as '*the fair-haired Iacint*', and not only for their scent and prettiness in the garden but also because their bulbs contained a gummy slime used for starching the linen ruffs and collars and wristbands fashionable at the time. This earned them the name of Starch Lilies.

When the mode for starched linen passed, or an easier supply of starch was more readily available, the plants still had a special use in the Levant. Before writing was common a young man would declare himself by offering a posy of mixed flowers, and silent assent was given and understood if the girl picked one of the ubiquitous Grape Hyacinths and stuck it in the posy.

Some species also make a delicious vegetable though doubts have been expressed as to the desirability of eating certain of the fifty-odd species which grow in the Mediterranean region. *M. comosum* is certainly safe and is grown as a vegetable in North Africa and South Italy. Cultivation adds greatly to the length of the flower-spike, the glossiness of the leaves, and the size of the pink bulb which is harvested in late spring. Most are pickled and preserved in oil for eating during the year. Fresh bulbs are fried like onions and they have a tart, nutty flavour of their own. They are at their best boiled with salt, dried, then seethed in a little vinegar and scattered with sugar until a hot syrup forms. However, should it be impossible to obtain the pickles or fresh supplies from a reliable source, or should there be the slightest uncertainty in identifying the species out in the field, it would be prudent to recall that an old and unscientific yet descriptive name for the Grape Hyacinth was *Bulbus vomitorum*.

Plate 18

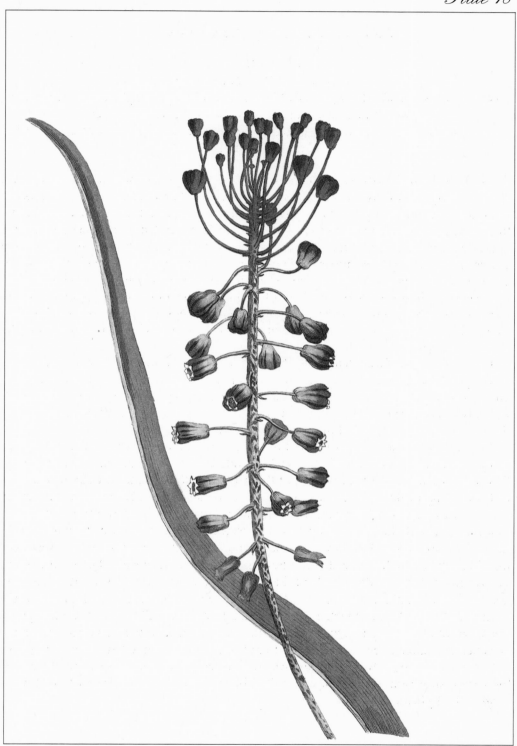

Muscari comosum

Rosa foetida Herrm.

AUSTRIAN ROSE, AUSTRIAN BRIAR

FAMILY: Rosaceae
SYNONYM: *Rosa lutea* Miller
DISTRIBUTION: central Europe, Asia Minor, Armenia, Iran, Afghanistan, Himalaya, North India (in Europe it is probably a garden escape)
CULTIVATION: hardy shrub; propagated by cuttings, layers, or seed; numerous garden varieties and hybrids

FOSSILS found in North America show the Rose to be older than man himself. Like the Lily it appears in the work of classical poets and historians, smiths and potters, gem-cutters and fresco-painters. It gave its name to the Greek island of Rhodes, and Roman senators debating confidential matters while garlanded with Roses gave us the expression *sub rosa*. In fact the plant has so long a lineage it is difficult to believe that any species now listed by nurserymen can fail to be the product of accidental matings before history began. As soon as records began to be made we read that some wild sorts were single, others double or many-petalled, and all had some sort of fragrance. There is no doubt the Romans cultivated and crossed them. Yet we still hold to the convention and put the yellow rose figured here as an introduction being grown by Gerard in 1596.

There is good field evidence that before then, as it is now, *R. foetida* was a wild species in Asia, and it probably entered Europe, as did so many other plants, in the diplomatic bag from the Sultan to the Holy Roman Emperor. For this reason the single yellow was called the Austrian Rose. The double yellow, named the Levant Rose, was shy of opening in a cooler climate than its native land.

To many people a Rose is the finest of all plants and its admirers form a vast cultus. They are by no means united. In fact few bodies of disciples are more disputatious. Devotees of what are called Species or Old-fashioned Roses, which are somewhat loose in form, delightfully scented, and have many romantic associations, have not much regard for those who have developed them and produced the modern Hybrid Teas and Floribundas, and their feelings are reciprocated. Both have a special interest in *R. foetida* because this rich yellow, almost fulvous oriental briar, probably a stabilized hybrid itself and highly regarded as a Species Rose, was the means whereby the colour yellow entered the modern Hybrid Teas, a delight to the hybridists but a source of dismay to the traditional lover of old Roses. It did not happen until 1900 when the French hybridist Pernet-Ducher produced the first 'Soleil d'Or', itself the five-greats grandparent of the famous Queen Elizabeth Rose. Since then the Pernetiana strain has enriched the range of colours available to hybridists so that they have everything from pale straw to orange. But the price paid was heavy: a great loss in fragrance, and an increasing susceptibility to a disease called Black Spot. The traditionalists will never forgive the hybridists for that.

Plate 19

Rosa foetida

Capparis spinosa L.

CAPER

FAMILY: Capparidaceae
SYNONYM: *Capparis rupestris* Sibth. & Smith
DISTRIBUTION: Mediterranean region
CULTIVATION: cool greenhouse plant; rarely flowers well in a pot; best planted out in light sandy soil or in rock or wall crevices; propagated by seed or by cuttings

THE closed buds of the Caper is the condiment used in sauces, not the highly poisonous fruit of the handsome Caper Spurge, *Euphorbia lathyrus*. Regrettable mistakes have frequently been made. The safe and pleasant-flavoured substitute for capers are Nasturtium seed pods, preferably harvested and pickled when green.

The plate shows the plant as it can often be seen growing, in bud and full flower and fruit. The green tear-shaped fruit on the right-hand side is a berry not yet ready to disseminate. As it ripens it alters, bellying out until it is much the shape and colour of a kestrel's egg. Dissected, the berries are seen to contain round brown seeds set in a sticky mass, and judging by the speed with which they propagate themselves a great many are viable and well dispersed. The beauty of the flower is in its delicacy. It is scented in strong sun. The sepals are a yellowish green, the almost diaphanous petals milk white flushed sometimes with rose, and the violet filaments with anthers at right angles resemble tiny hammerheads. In strong contrast to this delicacy are the glossy, almost leathery leaves and the firm buds, shown here at three stages of their development. They are usually picked at the first stage. Should they be only partly open they lose value commercially.

The plate only illustrates part of a small shrub which grows sometimes untidily but generally compactly to a height of a metre (3 feet). Nor does it show the rooting system, perhaps with good reason. In its native habitat either hanging pendantly in festoons or growing as a small shrub from cracks in limestone rock around the Mediterranean, the plant is so firmly rooted that a jemmy is required to prize it out. Therefore it is customarily harvested in the wild, pickers returning to each bush two or three times before the shrub is allowed to flower and fruit. In some places the Caper is cultivated. On the Italian Lipari Islands, for example, where the soil is volcanic, Caper seedlings are carefully trained until a permanent vegetative trunk is formed as thick and high as an umbrella stand. An experienced Caper farmer knows how many shoots he may allow to each parent and how many bud harvests he may take. Even then the fruits will generally be nipped off at an early stage so that the growing force may be returned to the advantage of the rooting system.

Plate 20

Capparis spinosa

Asphodeline lutea (L.) Reichenb.

YELLOW ASPHODEL, KING'S SPEAR

FAMILY: Liliaceae
SYNONYM: *Asphodelus luteus* L.
DISTRIBUTION: Mediterranean region and Orient
CULTIVATION: reasonably hardy perennial; prefers well-drained, sunny position;
propagated by division of the rootstock or by seed

ASPHODELINES and Asphodels differ because the former are rhizomatous and have leaves on their stems and the latter are tuberous and have a firework burst of basal leaves. Yet both, in a slapdash way, are commonly called Asphodels. A number of species of both genera grow in the Mediterranean maquis and, being so ubiquitous and so striking, they have found their way into literature, though not always with happy results. Farmers well know that the presence of Asphodels indicates poor soil or derelict ground, therefore we must suppose Homer was using poetic licence when he referred to a 'meadow' of Asphodels *'where dwell the souls, the phantoms of men outworn'*. Tennyson took up the theme writing crassly in *The Lotus Eaters* about *'resting weary limb at last on beds of Asphodel'*. Good poetry, yes; but horridly uncomfortable. A bed of lumpy, turgid Asphodels in growth would be only minimally more comfortable than a bed of the brittle, prickly sticks they become after flowering. But, then, in the same poem Tennyson wrote of the sweetness of lying *'propt on beds of amaranth and moly'* evidently unaware that Moly is a wild garlic which, under such pressure, would exude its stench in a pungent blast. Plants deserve more careful scrutiny from poets.

Gerard grew *Asphodeline lutea*, calling it the Yellow Asphodel. It has also been known as King's Spear and Jacob's Staff. Theophrastus, Dioscorides, and Pliny all said the succulent tubers or rhizomes of Asphodels were roasted in embers and eaten. At a later period Asphodel bread was made by boiling the dried roots in water to remove all trace of bitterness and mixing the result with grain or potato. Early botanists confirmed this, including Albrecht von Haller, an exact contemporary of Linnaeus who, with all respect to the great systematist, was far more distinguished intellectually but made less of a mark on the world because he confined his studies solely to the botany of Germany and his native Switzerland. Haller quoted authorities who maintained that the stem and the seeds as well as the roots were convertible into Asphodel bread. As recently as the Great War Asphodelines and Asphodels were eaten in Greece to ease the rationing restrictions. They have three other economic uses: the Algerians distil a pleasant liqueur from the roots; they are good forage for pigs and sheep; and, if the roots are first dried and afterwards mixed with water, they make a glue strong enough for bookbinding and cobbling shoes.

Plate 21

Asphodeline lutea

Mirabilis jalapa L.

MARVEL OF PERU, FOUR O'CLOCK PLANT,
BEAUTY OF THE NIGHT

FAMILY: Nyctaginaceae
DISTRIBUTION: warmer parts of America (probably originally from Mexico),
naturalized elsewhere
CULTIVATION: non-hardy perennial but often cultivated as a summer annual; thrives in
normal garden soil but needs a lot of water in summer, rootstocks should be lifted in
autumn; propagated by dividing the rootstock or by seed

SEVERAL species of *Mirabilis* were formerly garden favourites, their thick black tubers lifted each autumn and stored like Dahlias in sand. They were described in the most authoritative books and given such extravagant titles as '*The Mervaile of the World*'. Then their popularity dwindled. Now only one species, *M. jalapia*, is in general cultivation and it is treated as a half-hardy annual. Its English names are informative: Marvel of Peru indicates its provenance, the American tropics; Four o'clock Plant tells us that in bland climates the flowers open in the afternoon and stay open until the next morning.

On the whole plants are not considered as moving organisms unless they bend to wind or rain. In fact, though the majority stay in one position all are subject to growth changes. A few are not even static and actually move sideways through the soil, or heave themselves upwards through it like old bones in churchyards. And many plants show different kinds of movements in their different parts: for example, roots move towards water and food, tendrils and ripe seed vessels respond to touch, flowers move with the sun. Certain flowers, like the Crocus, Dandelion, and Scarlet Pimpernel, make what are called nastic movements, closing up if the sky becomes overcast, opening in the sun. The Four o'clock Plant's nastic movements are even more elaborate which gives a certain *cachet*. Its flowers are so light conscious that though, ordinarily, they close at dawn, they will remain open if the morning is dull. Moreover, the plant is only truly fragrant in the dark, its strongest scent being emitted at twilight.

The plate shows flowers of the most common colour but sometimes the trumpets are yellow or bright red or white or rose. Occasionally they are parti-coloured; one colour blotched with another, or a pair of colours arranged in neat stripes the length of the trumpet. The chief virtue of the flower, however, lies in its prodigality. It is on show from July until autumn, each flower being replaced by a five-sided vessel that changes from light green to jet black and hardens. These tough vessels that, like hazel nuts, contain one seed, are frequently used for rosary beads.

The Four o'clock Plant is the last of the 1596 introductions in this volume, dated thus because John Gerard listed them as growing in his garden at that date. Rogue though he might have been, he had an appreciative eye and a happy philosophy. '*Who would look up at the Planets*,' he asked, '*who could look down at Plants?*'

Plate 22

Mirabilis jalapa

Crocus angustifolius Weston

CLOTH OF GOLD CROCUS

FAMILY: Iridaceae
SYNONYMS: *Crocus susianus* Ker.-Gawl., *C. aureus* Sibth. & Smith
DISTRIBUTION: Balkans (Thrace), Asia Minor and Crimea
CULTIVATION: hardy corm; prefers exposed, well-drained slopes; propagated by corm offsets or by seed

CROCUSES grow all around the Mediterranean and the Levant and as far east as Afghanistan, and therefore it is not surprising to find the name in Hebrew and Sanscrit and Chaldean as well as in Greek and Latin. Commercially the most valuable Crocus is *C. sativus* because its dried, thread-like pistils are the saffron used as a dye, an aromatic flavouring, and a scent, and it takes thousands of flowers to produce only one pound of saffron. Horticulturally Crocuses are also important because careful selection and planting can ensure different species in bloom from late August until the following April.

The descriptively named Cloth of Gold Crocus originated from the north shores of the Black Sea and was introduced into cultivation in about 1597. At that early date Crocuses had not been sorted into categories and it was not until 1886 that an acceptable system was devised. Then because it flowered in early spring and because it had a tunic of membrane round its corm which resembled a vegetable net, this exquisite plant was thrust mundanely into Division II, Section I as though it were some sort of football or athletic team. But for three hundred years the Cloth of Gold always stood out as an exceptional species. The depth and intensity of its colours, the violet and orange and burnt umber, were particularly prized and, very soon after its introduction into cultivation, it was being grown and nurtured by Matthias de l'Obel, superintendent of the London physic garden of an enterprising plantsman and English nobleman, Lord Zouch. L'Obel, or Lobelius as he came to be known, was a young contemporary and compatriot of Clusius who shrewdly avoided the revolt in the Low Countries by crossing the Channel and lived in England for most of the rest of his life. He married an Englishwoman, supervised English gardens, and published floras, a book on cereals, and a treatise on the best methods of making English and German beer. He rose to become Botanist Royal but for long continued to superintend the garden of his first friend and patron Lord Zouch, where a variety of Crocuses was always a feature, the Cloth of Gold Crocus being the most highly regarded of all. Doubtless Lobelius would have thought it fitting to know that so lovely and widely popular a plant would one day give its name to an asteroid far out in space, and that of the 44,000 minor planets one is called Crocus.

Plate 23

Crocus angustifolius

Passiflora caerulea L.

COMMON PASSION FLOWER

FAMILY: Passifloraceae
DISTRIBUTION: sub-tropical and warm temperate regions of South America
CULTIVATION: climbing perennial that can withstand some frost, usually cultivated on sheltered south-facing walls or in a cool greenhouse, it can be cultivated as an annual; propagated by cuttings or by seed; several hybrids with *P. raddiana*, *P. racemosa*, and *P. alata*, and some garden forms known

THE earliest species of Passion Flower to be introduced into cultivation from its native Brazil was *P. caerulea*. This was certainly before the 17th century and it is still the best known and most widely grown. The Spanish and Portuguese missionaries to the Americas used its complicated flower structure to demonstrate to the natives the details of Christ's Passion. The ten white petals showed Our Lord's innocence; the outer circlet of purple filaments symbolized his countless disciples; the inner brown circlet his Crown of Thorns; the ovary was either the chalice he used at the Last Supper or the column to which he was tied, or the head of the hammer which drove in the nails; the five anthers were his wounds; the three divisions of the stigma the nails with which he was fastened to the Cross; and the tendrils represented the lashes of the scourging, just as the leaves were the hands of those who reached out to crucify him.

Because of its exotic appearance the Passion Flower attracted the attention of many artists during the great era of plant illustration and its introduction into cultivation was regarded as an event. Seeds were passed to botanists throughout Europe and, understandably, because the plant grew in the tropics, it was pampered as much as the limited skills of horticulture permitted. Quite a long time passed before it was discovered that the Passion Flower did not need to be spoilt, and in the 1870s it was still being recommended for the back wall or roof of an intermediate glasshouse. Even today it is cossetted and made much of as an evergreen house-plant. However, we now know that, though an exceptionally hard winter can cut it to the ground, it shoots again readily enough from the crown, and can be regarded as a hardy outdoor plant.

Some gardening writers have detected a fragrance which is fugitive to most noses and declare that its fruits are beautiful and edible. They are beautiful, and they may be edible, but they are not the highly esteemed Passion Fruit which is from another species, *P. edulis*.

Plate 24

Passiflora caerulea

Scilla peruviana L.

CORYMBOSE SQUILL, CUBAN LILY

FAMILY: Liliaceae
DISTRIBUTION: Mediterranean region
CULTIVATION: half-hardy bulb; does not flower well in pots, best planted out of doors
in summer; propagated by bulb offsets and by seed

Scilla peruviana is a good-looking plant that deserves a proper name for neither the botanic nor the common name is all that accurate.

There is a story that on a visit to England when he had the pleasure of meeting the circumnavigator, Sir Francis Drake, Clusius saw one of these plants down at the port of Bristol and because it had been brought to England in a ship named *Peru* he jumped to the wrong conclusion. There can be little truth in it. Clusius was not a nitwit. He must have been aware that there were plants very similar growing wild in the western Mediterranean region. Presumably, therefore, he considered the Bristol plant a solitary exotic specimen and not in cultivation. Whatever the truth of the matter, he named the plant *Hyacinthus stellatus peruvianus*. Linnaeus later renamed it a *Scilla* but unaccountably allowed himself to be misled into using the specific *peruviana*; and nobody has yet seen fit to correct the mistake. The first to cultivate it and say so in print was John Parkinson. He grew it before 1607 and called it the Great Spanish Starry Jacinth, which is fairly descriptive but rather too grandiose for ordinary use. The name used by some gardeners, Cuban Lily, is mischievously misleading. Squill would do, and is often used, but that was the name used by Theophrastus, Dioscorides, and Pliny for the Sea Squill, *Urginea maritima*, which has been used as a rat poison, in fertility rites, and in orthodox medical practice for two thousand years and more.

The plate gives some indication of the fleshiness of the plant but not its true size nor the stages of its development. The bulb is as big as a fine Spanish onion. When growth begins, pointed leaves form into a symmetric rosette. Then the star of leaves loosens and breaks up and each leaf, about 5 centimetres (2 inches) wide with a down along the margin, shoots up until it is more than 30 centimetres (a foot) long. The conical flower head when fully developed is as broad as it is high, about 12 centimetres by 12 (6 inches by 6); a conglomeration of anything up to a hundred flowers. Very rarely albino or mud-coloured varieties are found. Most often the species is a lively, clear blue deepening, as blue eyes do, with age.

Plate 25

Scilla peruviana

Zephyranthes atamasco (L.) Herb.

ATAMASCO LILY

FAMILY: Amaryllidaceae
SYNONYM: *Amaryllis atamasco* L.
DISTRIBUTION: south-eastern U.S.A., from Missouri and Virginia to Florida
CULTIVATION: coolhouse bulb; it can be placed outdoors in summer and brought indoors in winter, must be kept somewhat damp over winter; propagated by bulb offsets or by seed

THE first English settlement in North America was established in 1607 at Jamestown, now symbolically abandoned and left to moulder. The settlers took with them some important economic plants such as Wheat, which originated in south-west Asia, and Tobacco from South America. In return eastern North American plants found their way back across the Atlantic, either deliberately, a handful of seeds being taken home by a sailor or ship's surgeon or a returning missionary, or, more likely in those early days, quite by accident, from seeds in packing material or seeds blown aboard or carried aboard by the crew.

The plant figured here was one of the first to travel to Europe from the hunting grounds of the Powhatans, the Tuscaroras, and the Yamasees who allegedly ate the bulbs in times of scarcity. We accept the date of its introduction as before 1629 because John Parkinson was then growing it and calling it the Virginian Daffodil. The single flower is shapely and has a particularly lovely colouring. It is attractive at all stages from the time the bud emerges from its spathe until the six petals fold back to reveal the stamens within and the long protruding style and stigma. Neverthless it is generally upstanding, or only a few degrees from the vertical, which poses the question why for so long it was regarded as a Narcissus. It was thirty-three years after Parkinson's death and burial in St. Martin-in-the-Fields, London, that the plant was first called *Atamasco*. This was by a taciturn Scot named Morison, an undergraduate destined for Holy Orders who, unable to resist the excitement of the Civil War, rode off to fight and was banged on the head in battle. On recovery he emigrated, studied medicine and natural history, and quickly rose to the top of his profession becoming Senior Physician and Gardener to King Charles II and first Professor of Botany at Oxford. There he began listing the plants growing in the Botanic Garden. Among them was what he called a *Lilio-narcissus*, noting 'Atamasco dictus'. He never, however, saw his work in print, being knocked down by a coach shaft in a London street and banging his head on the cobblestones. This time he did not recover. He, too, was buried in St. Martin-in-the-Fields. Seventy-three years after that Linnaeus named the plant *Amaryllis atamasco*, but, though a member of the Amaryllidaceae, it was not an Amaryllis. Eventually the name *Zephyranthes* was concocted from the Greek words for west wind and flower. It is appropriate for so early an introduction from the West to the Old World.

Plate 26

Zephyranthes atamasco

Ipomoea purpurea (L.) Roth.

PURPLE BINDWEED, MORNING GLORY

FAMILY: Convolvulaceae
SYNONYM: *Convolvulus purpureus* L., *Pharbitis purpurea* (L.) Voigt
DISTRIBUTION: tropical America
CULTIVATION: annual twiner; prefers a sunny position; several garden varieties

THIS plate has two features in common with the preceding one: it figures an early arrival from the warm temperate part of the North American littoral and it was first cultivated and written up by John Parkinson in 1629. One of its English names, Morning Glory, indicates it is not ordinarily a long-lasting flower, though in a bland climate it will continue flowering, less gloriously perhaps, well into the afternoon.

Parkinson could have only hazarded a guess as to how many species of plants there were in the world. One hundred years after him Linnaeus estimated that the total was not likely to exceed 10,000. At the latest count it is in the region of 225,000, divided into anything up to 12,500 genera. This gives an average of 18 species to a genus. Therefore it is remarkable to consider the size of the Ipomoea clan. It has more than 500 species, and close relatives of the Morning Glory are the Moonvine of the tropics; Porter's Joy, an American species that has crept along all the railway lines of India; Jalap; the Chinese Cabbage of tropical Asia; the Imperial Morning Glories so cherished a hundred years ago in Japan that single seeds fetched the price of semi-precious stones; and that valuable source of human food, alcohol, and animal fodder, the Sweet Potato. It is notable that some are trees but the majority are twiners, a great number evergreen, but some are annuals like *I. purpurea*.

In hot, baking conditions Morning Glories can be as invasive as the Bindweeds of temperate climates, and they will not only twine clockwise up the nearest support, and even, improbably, round each other like coupling serpents if there is nothing else to scramble up, but they will also sprawl and run over the earth and dangle from rocks looking for places to attach themselves. Mostly gardeners train the plant over fences or up trelliswork, but perhaps they are best of all grown in a large pot, either in a greenhouse, or light garden room, or even in the protection of a wall, and allowed to clamber over a large birdcage structure of bamboo canes. There are many colour varieties, the most striking a scarlet veined with violet that, as the morning passes, lightens to Bishop's purple.

An interesting historical point about this plate is that chronologically it was the last issued by William Curtis from his garden in Lambeth Marsh situated somewhere between the River Thames and the present site of Waterloo Station. The next was issued from his new garden in Brompton.

Plate 27

Ipomoea purpurea

Briza maxima L.

GREE T QUAKING GRASS

FAMILY: Graminae
SYNONYM: *Briza major*
DISTRIBUTION: Mediterranean region, naturalized elsewhere
CULTIVATION: half-hardy annual; prefers a sunny position

GERARD made or pirated quite a number of errors in his *Herball* of 1597 and when it was known that John Parkinson, the Botanist Royal, intended to issue a second authoritative herbal entitled *Theater of Plants*, the printer who held Gerard's stolen plates decided to forestall him, rush through a corrected and larger edition of the herbal, and steal Parkinson's thunder. He chose a young apothecary named Thomas Johnson to bring Gerard's *Herball* up to date, and gave him a bare twelve months in which to do it. Johnson managed it. But then he was a vigorous and enterprising man, famed for being the first to show Londoners a bunch of Bananas; famed for his energetic botanical expeditions going even to Wales where he climbed Mount Snowdon and arranged the plants he had collected on the cloud-shrouded summit; and sadly famed for an heroic death at the early age of 44 whilst in command of a besieged Royalist house in the Civil War. No less fame ought to be attached to him for doctoring and prinking out and adding to Gerard's 1,630 pages within a year. It was a remarkable achievement. In it he included the Mediterranean Quaking Grass, and therefore the date of the book's publication, 1633, is taken as the date of its introduction into cultivation.

It is not surprising that later the plant should have been chosen for illustration in the *Botanical Magazine*. The leaflets, the slender stems, and the nodding oval flower spikelets are all highly admirable, especially the last. Indeed, their overlapping, chaffy segments are so ingeniously constructed that they resemble the scales of articulated fish fashioned by goldsmiths as brooches and pendants. Though an annual the grass is a free seeder and will soon make a colony in protected places. Possibly, however, it is best appreciated growing from a rough wall or embankment where it can be seen from below.

The art of flower-arranging, while older than written history in the Orient, is mostly supposed to be a 19th or 20th century innovation in the Occident and that enlightened lady decorators have at last discovered the beauty of Grasses. William Curtis in his letterpress on the Quaking Grass explodes this theory. '*They have a twofold claim, as they not only decorate the garden when fresh, but the mantleshelf when dry; to these purposes the present species of Briza has long been applied.*'

Plate 28

Briza maxima

Lavatera trimestris L.

ANNUAL LAVATERA

FAMILY: Malvaceae
SYNONYMS: *Lavatera alba* Medic, *L. rosea* Medic
DISTRIBUTION: Mediterranean region
CULTIVATION: hardy summer annual; numerous garden varieties

THE 18th century Lavater family of Zurich, for whom Linnaeus named the genus, had distinguished members, naturalists and physicians of high repute and, perhaps the most widely known, Johann Kaspar the poet, physiognamist, and mystical writer who for a time was an intimate of Goethe. Their friendship diminished at almost exactly the same speed as Lavater's high opinion of himself ballooned. He became so swanky that in his fifties all Zurich ridiculed him, and he only redeemed himself in the eyes of his fellow citizens when the French seized Zurich in 1799 and he bravely tried to calm a riotous group of grenadiers. One of them promptly shot him through the body which caused him excruciating and increasing pain until he died in agony, an acclaimed patriot, eighteen months afterwards.

The plant's second name, *trimestris*, tells us it is an annual and worth garden space for three months. It can reach 120 centimetres (4 feet) in height and, well fed, blooms profusely, its flowers measuring 10 to 12 centimetres (4 or 5 inches) in diameter. The depth of its rose colour depends largely on the type of soil in which it grows. In its wild native state in Mediterranean countries, it is one of the most robust and fastest-growing of all annuals. Theoretically introduced in 1633 because Thomas Johnson included it in the revised Gerard's *Herball* of that date, it has always done well in temperate climates, making a good show of deeply-veined leaves and colour and is admirably suited for gathering as a cut flower. It somewhat resembles its relatives the Hibiscus and the Hollyhock, and at one time it showed the latter's susceptibility to the rust fungus. Now, however, its chief enemies are leaf spot, for which there is no satisfactory cure, and green Peach-potato Aphids which can be controlled by toxic sprays but are better and more economically dealt with by ladybirds, hoverflies, and lace-wings, and a minute parasite which lays eggs in the aphid like a blowfly in a cow; once these are hatched they commence to eat the pest alive until it is a mere shell.

Plate 29

Lavatera trimestris

Aquilegia canadensis L.

CANADIAN COLUMBINE

FAMILY: Ranunculaceae
DISTRIBUTION: eastern North America
CULTIVATION: hardy perennial; propagated by dividing the rootstock or by seed;
readily hybridizes with other species. 'Pure' *Aquilegia canadensis* is very rarely seen in
gardens today

THE Tradescants were a unique trio of 17th century East Anglian gardeners and antiquaries; father, son, and grandson; all Christened John and all remembered in one epitaph that mentions their 'Transplanting' to a better world, and ends:

*– these thence shall rise
And change their gardens for a Paradise*

The first John was a collector of foreign plants in Central Europe, Russia, and on the Barbary Coast. The second was collecting in the infant colony of Virginia when his father died in 1637 and he returned to succeed him as royal gardener, and bring, among other plants, the Canadian Columbine here figured.

Aquilegia has its name from the Latin for an eagle as the flowers are supposed to resemble that bird. It seems far fetched. Much better is the English name Columbine from *columba*, a dove, because on examining a hanging flower the five honey spurs above the sepals look exactly like five doves with their heads together billing and cooing. This is particularly true of *A. vulgaris*, the blue or dull Lenten mauve common European Columbine, with the medieval reputation that it was a delicacy in the diet of lions. Its honeyed spurs are exceedingly hooked. In *A. canadensis* they are less so, though they still bear some resemblance to birds with their heads together, and their numerous stamens, often 50 or more, are much longer than those of the common Columbine. They are pollinated by humble-bees. Unfortunately, the genus is very fecund and has crossed and re-crossed, and if the common Columbine is about it dominates most other species. As a result a seed packet of a named strain is gardener's roulette. Nevertheless the plant is worth a gamble, and if John Tradescant's Virginian Columbine springs up so much the better. The sight of its yellow and red sepals and petals nodding and bobbing under the weight of a hairy, brightly marked humble-bee is like a moving kaleidoscope of colour.

Plate 30

Aquilegia canadensis

Teucrium fruticans L.

SHRUBBY GERMANDER, TREE GERMANDER

FAMILY: Labiatae
DISTRIBUTION: western Mediterranean to southern Italy
CULTIVATION: half-hardy perennial; simple to keep in a cool greenhouse or can be kept
out of doors in frost-free places; propagated by cuttings

THE genus *Teucrium* is so widely spread that botanists agree it is subcosmopolitan, possibly even cosmopolitan. It has a name first used by Dioscorides in honour of Teucer, a legendary king of Phrygia, who gave his name to the Teucri or Trojans who used plants medicinally.

T. fruticans, the Tree Germander, is indigenous to the Mediterranean littoral and was first mentioned by John Parkinson in his second herbal, *Theater of Plants*. This book, though some of its thunder had been stolen by the reprinting of an improved Gerard's *Herball*, was still a worthy and lasting work that covered much ground; gardening, plant lists, plant lore, medicinal and household receipts, and even the preservation of mummies. It was the last of the important English herbals for all that followed it were shot through with astrology, the doctrine of signatures, witchcraft, quackery, and a great deal of nonsense. Its publication in 1640 is taken as the date of the Germander's introduction into cultivation. It was a year of accomplishments, the first American book being printed in Massachusetts Bay Colony, coke was first made from coal, large lakes and fenlands were drained in Holland and England, the first café as we know it was opened in Vienna, and Rembrandt painted his self-portrait.

Though members of the lipped Mint family, Tree Germanders have no noticeable upper lip but the lower one is pronounced and divided into five sections, the third being by far the largest. The protruding style and stamens make the flowers look like long-tailed moths. The colour varies from a clear sky blue to, more rarely, a dusty ultramarine. Equally attractive are the egg-shaped leaves, olive to grey above, and white felted beneath.

Left to itself the plant will grow to a bush 120 centimetres (4 feet) high, and this is how it is seen in its native habitat. It does, however, respond to topiary and for many years Germanders have been grown as a clipped hedging plant on the French and Italian Riviera. Correctly they bloom in spring and early summer, but they also have generous bursts of flowering at unseasonable times.

Plate 31

Teucrium fruticans

Phytolacca americana L.

POKEWEED, PIGEON-BERRY

FAMILY: Phytolaccaceae
DISTRIBUTION: North America, naturalized elsewhere
CULTIVATION: large perennial herb that does not withstand severe frosts; propagated by dividing the rootstock or by seed

POKEWEED was introduced to Europe from the European settlements in North America and was well established in cultivation by 1640. To a certain extent its height is determined by its habitat but it is a sturdy perennial even in the Old World. And thus we are shown details by the artist who figured its leaf, flower, and fruit. The author of the letterpress accompanying this trim plate wrote: '*It may be observed that it has rather a suspicious aspect.*' This is a curious comment as Pokeweed does not look in the least sinister. It is only after reading a number of conflicting reports that we realize the writer must have been prejudiced by the plant's reputation. Unravelled, the facts show it had and still has utilities.

In all its parts, but at different strengths, Pokeweed contains an emetic which is also narcotic. Therefore as a medical herb it has to be handled capably or not at all. The dried fleshy roots were used as a purge by the Indian and Pennsylvanian Dutch, and the former, being so much out of doors and prone to rheumatism, early discovered that the herb could be used as an alleviant. The greatest relief was obtained by a primitive form of sweat bath incorporating Pokeweed; the easiest, used by the Pamunkey Indians of Virginia, by drinking a brew of the boiled berries. The berries have also been used as chicken food, though, like deliberate arsenic eaters, the fowls gradually gain an immunity to the drug while their flesh still has an emetic effect on human beings even after roasting. The dried root has been ground up and used for a variety of ailments, as well as a cattle drench and a slug-killer. The juice, too, has been used medicinally, and for a long time, until the wine merchants complained of the taste, as a dye to deepen the colour of port. Thereafter, because virtually no such thing as 'pure' port exists, elderberries were used for colouring the wine, molasses for sweetening it, and silent spirit as a fortifier. The plant's most common use is as a green spring vegetable but only when it is in first growth and small, about 45 centimetres (18 inches) high. Then the shoot and the top five or six felted leaves of each plant, complete with the rose-coloured leaf stems, are gathered. Possibly Pokeweed is too commonly seen to be appreciated in its native North America. In Europe it is still grown for gourmets, boiled for a quarter of an hour in two lots of water, drained, and served on toasted wholegrain bread, sauced with clarified butter.

Plate 32

Phytolacca americana

Sprekelia formosissima (L.) Herb.

JACOBEAN AMARYLLIS, OR LILY

FAMILY: Amaryllidaceae
SYNONYM: *Amaryllis formosissimum* L.
DISTRIBUTION: Mexico and Guatemala
CULTIVATION: non-hardy bulb; a greenhouse plant or it can be placed outdoors during the summer and brought indoors in winter, from late summer to mid-winter it must be kept dry; propagation by bulb offsets or by seed

JUST as there may be a difference between the date of a plant being known to exist and the date of its introduction into cultivation, so there is sometimes a clear distinction between attempted and successful introduction. The case of the Jacobean Lily is a clear example of the latter.

The *Botanical Magazine* states that, according to Linnaeus, the plant was first known in Europe in 1593. Next in order we are told that Clusius wrote the plant up in 1601, presumably as an exceptional exotic not in general cultivation. Then Parkinson put it in his *Paradisi* of 1629 under the long-winded name 'Indian Daffodil with the Red Flower'. This may be accounted as the date of its first introduction but, because the bulb was tender and the exceedingly few greenhouses in existence were unheated and admitted no more light than the chapels they so closely resembled, it was not successful. Therefore the date 1658, when we know it was growing plentifully in the Oxford Botanic Garden, is accepted as the date of its successful introduction.

At Oxford it was wintered in a conservatory heated by a wheeled brazier of glowing charcoal pulled backwards and forwards by a gardener's boy, a building of such solid construction that two hundred years afterwards it was easily transformed into a library and a private house. Such substantial stone greenhouses and orangeries were soon outmoded, and even glazing and cast-iron girders have given place to plastic sheeting over light supports so that the Jacobean Lily may be grown by anyone and everyone.

The Lily is a native of southern Mexico and Guatemala; and in the wild its colour can vary from pink through velvet crimson marked with white to the shade of a Savoy cabbage; while some plants are evergreen and some deciduous. All are fair game to the 'splitters' who like lots of sub-names for their plants. The fact remains that it is a solitary beauty, being a genus with only one species. In cultivation it is deciduous and like some other Amaryllids throws up its long, ribbon, grass-green leaves after it has flowered. The mauve stem is hollow, the dark bulb round and long-necked like a small bottle gourd.

Plate 33

Sprekelia formosissima

Liriodendron tulipifera L.

TULIP TREE, WHITEWOOD

FAMILY: Magnoliaceae
DISTRIBUTION: eastern North America
CULTIVATION: hardy tree; grows in a wide variety of conditions but prefers deep loam and some shelter; propagated by seed, or choice varieties can be grafted on *Liriodendron* seedlings

HERE is a plate that ought to be introduced with a fanfare of silver trumpets. The Tulip Tree not only has very special aesthetic qualities, but is also an important economic plant and of great interest to the plant historian and plant geographer.

Well named from the Greek for lily and tree, it flowers in the high summer and, except for the three fallen sepals and its powerful fragrance, it closely resembles a tulip. The leaf, which is unique in the vegetable world, appears to have been snipped or bitten off, and it has a bat-winged look. The plate is a small detail of one of the largest of deciduous trees, and at one time of the year. After fertilization the cone-shaped, compound pistil disintegrates into dozens of winged fruits which the wind blows over a considerable area. Then the leaves turn yolk-yellow before falling. In winter the tree has a handsome skeleton and the winter buds are pointed, borne on short stalks arranged spirally round the twigs, and each bud is sheathed by two protective scales.

It is believed the second John Tradescant introduced the tree to Europe on one or other of the three expeditions he made to North America in 1637, 1642 and 1654, and there it is grown solely for ornamental purposes, reaching a height up to 35 metres (100 feet). In its native America it can reach 65 metres (190 feet) and is often grown as a good shade tree as well as for timber. It makes a columnar trunk of 2.5 to 3 metres (8 to 9 feet) in diameter with grey, aromatic bark, and though its yellowish, smooth, fine-grained wood is not very strong, it is easy to work and does not split. Therefore it is in great demand by cabinet-makers. But this is not all. Its inner bark is the source of a heart stimulant used in orthodox medical practice. Finally, the genus has only two species, one of which grows in eastern North America, and the other, a similar but smaller tree, which was found in eastern China as recently as 1901. It is therefore a striking example of what botanists call discontinuity; that is, the phenomenon of a genus being oceans apart in its distribution. Equally inexplicable and weird is the fact that in pre-history its areas of distribution were quite different. Those unmistakable leaves have been found in fossils which show that millions of years ago Tulip Trees were indigenous to Iceland, the south of England, Central Europe, and Italy, and to Japan, not China, and to areas in the west not the east of North America. It falls within the scope of what Darwin called 'an abominable mystery'.

Plate 34

Liriodendron tulipifera

Arisaema triphyllum (L.) Torry

JACK-IN-THE-PULPIT

FAMILY: Araceae
SYNONYM: *Arum triphyllum* L.
DISTRIBUTION: eastern North America from Carolina to Canada
CULTIVATION: the true wild species should be a hardy perennial but it is usually cultivated in a cool greenhouse; propagated by corm offsets or by seed

JOHN Evelyn was an excellent example of the cultured 17th century Englishman, a man of sweet disposition and acute mind; a founder member of the Royal Society, well travelled and widely read; a distinguished writer and a passionate collector of 'curious greens'. In 1664 he was growing a fascinating introduction from America where the British had just seized New Amsterdam and renamed it New York. This was the tiger-striped Aroid, *Arisaema triphyllum*. Arisaemas look like their cousins the Arums but they differ because Arisaema flower spikes are either male or female but never both. Yet their sex can be altered capriciously at will. All a gardener has to do is change the fertility of the plant's surroundings. A female growing in rich soil becomes male in barren land. Equally intriguing is the fact that the flower is pollinated by a single species of insect trapped for the night within the spathe, and for some strange reason 99 per cent of the insects are female. Moreover, the mature plant reproduces itself not only by seed dispersal but also vegetatively from daughter tubers springing from the parent, and a colony is established by parents and daughters that move, mole-fashion, through friable soil as much as 2.5 centimetres (1 inch) in a year. For centuries both Arisaemas and Arums were regarded as an aphrodisiac, but most contain a poison, and only a few failing lovers can have survived to enjoy fresh potency. What happened to those who took the precarious preparations prescribed by physicians until the plant was taken from the pharmacopoeia can only be imagined. Boiling reduced some of the poison and ground-up Arisaema tubers have been used like arrowroot, and for cosmetics, and as a source of starch. But never has the acrid principle been entirely eliminated. The wearers of starched ruffs often found themselves with inflamed necks. The earthy English called the plant Cuckoopint, from the Anglo-Saxon words meaning 'a lively male member', but it has been less bawdily described as Soldiers and Angels and Lords and Ladies, and poetically by Thomas Hardy as '*an apoplectic saint in a niche of malachite*'. By far the most common and descriptive is used on both sides of the Atlantic, Jack- or Parson-in-the-Pulpit. The plate demonstrates that here is a parson so tiny and modest he does not even peer over the side of his pulpit. As if to make up for his littleness the top of the spathe is hooded and turns over to give him a sounding-board.

Plate 35

Arisaema triphyllum

Agapanthus africanus (L.) Hoffmgg.

AFRICAN AGAPANTHUS, BLUE LILY

FAMILY: Liliaceae
SYNONYMS: *Agapanthus orientalis* Auct., *A. umbellatus* L'Hérit.
DISTRIBUTION: southern and eastern parts of South Africa
CULTIVATION: half-hardy plants with fleshy rootstocks; usually cultivated in pots that are placed outdoors in summer and kept in a cool frost-free place in winter, it should not be repotted too frequently as the thick roots hate disturbance; propagated by dividing the rootstock

THE Agapanthus is a gift from Africa, brought first from the Cape of Good Hope by an unknown traveller and introduced into cultivation in 1679. The plant was so highly thought of that fresh stocks were sought for, and, within a dozen years, plants were being grown all over Europe. Then gardeners began to notice that some specimens appeared to be taller and to have more flowers than others. This was puzzling as they fully believed the African Lily was monotypic; that is, a genus of species. With the advantage of hindsight we can see two possible reasons for the differences. It might have been because the plants hybridized promiscuously and crossed varieties sprang up differing from the type. Or it could have been because the fresh plants or seeds imported to meet the high public demand were, in fact, different species. At any rate, with the passage of time there was such an orgy of crossing and re-crossing in the world of garden Agapanthuses that it led to confusion. Apart from variations in size and colour and numbers of flowers, some were evergreen and others deciduous, and some freaks put out extra flowers from the side of the umbel (called 'hen and chickens') and others put out extras from the top (called 'pagodas'). Only very recent work has established that, besides the garden illegitimates, between 5 and 10 species with their subspecies can properly be named.

The plate almost certainly illustrates the evergreen *A. africanus*. It is smaller than most African Lilies, between 46 and 61 centimetres (1½ and 2 feet), with more leathery leaves, and seldom has more than a dozen dense, waxy flowers. The Common Agapanthus, now called *A. praecox* ssp. *orientalis*, grows to between 1 and 1.2 metres (3 and 4 feet) and has a densely crowded umbel of more than 150 flowers that vary in colour from light blue to dark. The flowers of *A. africanus* are a deep blue with a darker stripe, though this can vary in intensity depanding on how much the plant is watered. North of the Equator it is in bloom in September and October; south, from December to March. It is unique amongst Agapanthuses in that it needs abundant watering in winter and scarcely any at all in summer.

Plate 36

Agapanthus africanus

Tropaeolum majus L.

GREATER INDIAN CRESS, NASTURTIUM

FAMILY: Tropaeoliaceae
DISTRIBUTION: South and Central America
CULTIVATION: in the wild state it is an orange-flowered, perennial climber, the garden
varieties are probably hybrids of *Tropaeolum majus* with *T. peltophorum* and *T. minus*,
they are cultivated today as half-hardy annuals

SEEDS of *T. minus*, a compact, non-climbing variety, were distributed through Europe from Spain in the 16th century. Lobelius wrote it up in 1576 and it was well liked by both Gerard and Parkinson, the latter remarking that it made '*a delicate Tussiemussie, as they call it, or Nosegay, both for sight and scent*'. However, the more familiar climbing Nasturtium here figured was not introduced to Europe from South America until 1684. In cultivation its natural orange flowers began to throw rogues of different colours and it became very popular, so much so that *T. minus* virtually disappeared and had to be reintroduced in the 18th century.

All parts of all species of *Tropaeolum* contain a tasty mustard oil reminiscent to Europeans of Watercress, *Nasturtium officinale*. Hence the English names Nasturtium and Indian Cress, and the use of its leaves and stems and flowers in salads, the pickling of its flower buds and young green fruits. John Evelyn, who was something of an epicure as well as a knowledgeable plantsman, reckoned that mustard made from finely ground dried Nasturtium seeds had the best flavour of all. The tubers of two species, *T. tuberosum* and *T. leptophyllum*, can be boiled and eaten, and have a hottish cress taste. From a dietary point of view the plants are important being rich in vitamin C.

Linnaeus chose the generic name, indulging himself in a flight of classical fancy. In his day gardeners grew *T. majus* up sticks so that they made columns of colour. Linnaeus saw a likeness to the tropaeum set up by Roman legionaries on the field of battle decorated with the arms of their enemies; the leaves resembling shields, and the flowers golden helmets streaked with blood. Apparently his daughter Christina permitted herself another, as yet undemonstrated fancy that at sunset Nasturtium flowers gave off electrical sparks. Goethe is said to have had the same acute powers of observation. No one else has. More recently it has been alleged that the tart oil of Nasturtiums is offensive to aphids and therefore it is worth growing them in greenhouses and up the boles of fruit trees to control these pests.

Plate 37

Tropaeolum majus

Plumeria rubra L.

RED PLUMERIA, FRANGIPANI, WEST INDIAN JASMINE

FAMILY: Apocynaceae
DISTRIBUTION: West Indies and Central America from Mexico to Panama
CULTIVATION: a small tree for the heated greenhouse where the temperature should not fall below 16°C.; after flowering it should not be watered for a month or two; it rarely blooms satisfactorily in cultivation. It is propagated by stem cuttings; the cuttings should be left for their wounds to heal before planting

IN the faulting and upheavals and flooding during the 150 million years or so that flowering plants have been growing, North and South America have been disconnected and a great mountain range from Honduras to Trinidad has been inundated so that only the peaks now stand out as the islands of the West Indies. Considering this, it is remarkable how rich the region is in its flora. Two men share the honour of being the fathers of West Indian botany. The lesser important was Sir Hans Sloane, 1660–1753, a long-lived Irish physician who was in the Antilles for fifteen months. Fractionally more important was Charles Plumier (1646–1704), a Frenchman who became a Minime friar and was sent thrice by his Order as a missionary to the West Indies and botanized as he catechized. It was he who reverted to the Greek custom of naming genera after people who deserved the compliment. Therefore it was meet that Linnaeus, in following his example, should name the lovely tree figured here after Plumier who found it in Haiti.

The genus has seven species, the best known being the fragrant *P. rubra* which, since its first introduction into cultivation at some time before 1690, has been a popular stove plant. An old manuscript exists which describes a tour made by a Mr J. Gibson of a number of gardens in and around London in January 1691. Evidently by then the art of wintering tender plants had moved a step forwards. In the gardens of Hampton Court there was '*a large greenhouse divided into several rooms, and all of them with stoves under them, and fire to keep a continual heat*'. It contained a thriving *P. rubra*. The tree has also been widely planted in the tropics right round the world and not only for ornamental purposes. Its sap makes a good drawing poultice and the Indonesians use the flowers in cooking. More important, because of its apparent resistance to death, Buddhists, Hindus, and Muslims associate the tree with immortality. Cuttings left to dry for a long time will strike if they are put in a rooting compost. A broken-off branch will temporarily continue to leaf and bud and even blossom like Aaron's rod. For this reason it is frequently planted near graves in the East, and close to temples so that the funnel-shaped flowers can be gathered as offerings.

Plate 38

Plumeria rubra

Cotyledon orbiculata L.

ROUND-LEAVED NAVAL-WORT, PIG'S EAR

FAMILY: Crassulaceae
DISTRIBUTION: South Africa
CULTIVATION: non-hardy herb or subshrub; suitable for a cool greenhouse but should
be kept dry during the winter; propagated by stem or leaf cuttings or by seed; it is
variable and readily hybridizes with other species

THE pioneer of South African botany was a Dutch clergyman-physician named
Justus Heurnius who called at the Cape of Good Hope on his way to or from the then
Dutch colonies in India and Ceylon and wrote up and illustrated a number of plants he
found growing there. Eight of his drawings were included in a commentary on
Theophrastus written by a fellow naturalist and published in 1644, and in this odd
way the first account of Cape plants was presented to the world. Amongst the eight
was a figure of *C. orbiculata*. On account of the appearance of its leaves the plant picked
up the name of Pig's Ear, but it was not actually introduced into cultivation for another
forty-six years. Then, like the Agapanthus which preceded it to Europe, nothing is
known of the person who introduced it save that he was under the patronage of the Earl
of Portland. Why Pig's Ear was not introduced until 1690 is a mystery, especially as –
vermin permitting – succulents stood the best chance of surviving the voyage, being by
nature accustomed to long spells of drought and having reservoirs of water in their
fleshy parts. Once introduced, cultivation was a matter of experiment, and eventually
it was decided that Pig's Ear was only half-hardy. This is another mystery. At the
Cape of Good Hope it could and does withstand several degrees of frost. Possibly it is
because, like many other African succulents which are less adaptable than their
American cousins, Cotyledons have never adjusted themselves to being carried over
the equator and what they will tolerate at the Cape they cannot tolerate in Canton,
Cracow, or Connecticut. In the northern hemisphere they rest in summer and grow in
the winter.

The two details shown in the plate emphasize the plant's height, the tallest part
being the drooping flower trumpets. When the oval leaves are gorged with water they
appear green and glistening. At normal times they are stone grey and mealy with a thin
scarlet line along the edge. Always they are poisonous. There are several varieties in
the wild. Only two are grown in cool houses and rockeries, the one figured in the plate,
and another with smaller egg-shaped leaves that feel exactly like the fleshy lobes of a
human ear and have the memorable name *C.o.* 'Oophylla'.

Plate 39

Cotyledon orbiculata

Canaria canariensis (L.) Mansf.

CANARY BELL-FLOWER

FAMILY: Campanulaceae

DISTRIBUTION: Canary Islands

CULTIVATION: half-climbing perennial; needs a heated greenhouse, the rootstock must be kept dry during the summer; propagated by careful division of the rootstock just before it sprouts (usually in August) or by seed, but they take at least three years to bloom

PLANT geographers have been obliged to divide the globe into floristic regions. It has always been an arbitrary business. For example, in 1823 J. F. Schouw carved the world into twenty-five vegetable kingdoms, and it has been done several times since. Indeed this sort of classification is a living thing in great botanical libraries such as that at Kew where it is possible to overhear authorities argue whether a tiny coral atoll ought to be in 19e or 19f and come to no definite conclusion. However, there is a general degree of unanimity and it has been agreed that the Canary Islands, the home of the unusual red flower figured in the plate, is in the Macaronesian Region of the Boreal Kingdom. The Azores, Madeira, and Cape Verdes are in the same group and, considering how small the total land surface is compared with, say, the Sino-Japanese region, it is remarkable how many species are endemic there. All were well explored botanically at an early period as they lay in the trade routes, and the Canary Bell Flower was established in the Hampton Court stove by 1696. Probably it would have been in cultivation before had it not required a greenhouse and a little extra warmth at the critical time of flowering.

Interestingly there are only three species of the genus; two of them, despite the generic name, endemic to a region of Africa from Ethiopia to Tanzania, the third, *C. canariensis*, endemic to only four islands in the whole of the archipelago. It belongs to the Campanula family but, unlike an ordinary Campanula which has five points to its bell, its bronze and scarlet striped bell has six. It even has a clapper, an orange club-shaped pistil. The tooth-edged leaves vary in shape, some resembling ivy, others grapevines. The light green veining on sepals and leaves is as neat and fine as the nerve stripes of the flower. The fruit is an edible berry.

This plate of the Canary Bell-flower published in May 1779 was one of the last issued by the founder of the *Botanical Magazine*. William Curtis died that July leaving a daughter as proprietor. One of his brothers, Thomas Curtis, looked after the magazine for the next two years.

Plate 40

Canaria canariensis

Rubus odoratus L.

FLOWERING RASPBERRY, THIMBLEBERRY

FAMILY: Rosaceae
DISTRIBUTION: central and southern North America
CULTIVATION: hardy shrub up to 3 metres (9 feet) tall; prefers fresh soil and half
shade; propagated by suckers, cuttings, or seed

THE genus *Rubus* is gigantic. It has at least 250 species spread over the face of the earth, and what to the layman is merely a common Blackberry, *R. fructicosus*, has been the subject of tireless study by botanical 'splitters' who have found more than 3,000 kinds that are fractionally different from each other. Some species are endemic to North America where the prickly plants are called Blackberries and the rest Raspberries.

The species figured, *R. odoratus*, the Flowering Raspberry, has fruit that appeals chiefly to birds and children. To most palates it tastes of nothing at all. Still, since it grows to about 3 metres (9 feet), has an abundance of pretty, fragrant flowers, and makes few demands on a gardener, it is worth growing. Like other species in the genus it has been attributed with healing powers for a variety of complaints such as tightening loose teeth and easing globular eyeballs. There is some speculation about the date of its introduction into cultivation. Very probably it was effected by Sir Hans Sloane who was cultivating it in London in 1700. As was often the way with learned men at that time Sloane had read medicine at Paris, botany at Montpellier, and graduated M.D. at the University of Orange. He went out to Jamaica in 1687 as physician to the newly appointed Governor but his patient slipped without warning into the next world. Only a few days after their arrival, Sloane took the opportunity to make botanical explorations of the islands collecting more than 800 specimens in fifteen months. He returned to London in May 1689, bought the Manor of Chelsea, established a physic garden there, and settled in general practice with great success. Distinction piled upon distinction. He was made a baronet and Physician-in-Ordinary to the King, followed Sir Isaac Newton as President of the Royal Society, and when he died at the great age of 93 his natural history collections, together with his library and his notes, became the basis of the British Museum. Number 3359 of the Sloane Manuscripts refers to *R. odoratus*, the American Flowering Raspberry. A commentator remarked that Sloane Street named after him in London was exactly like his life, 'straight, elegant and long'.

Plate 41

Rubus odoratus

Lathyrus odoratus L.

SWEET PEA

FAMILY: Leguminosae
DISTRIBUTION: confined to southern Italy and Sicily
CULTIVATION: hardy annual, that requires much light and a loose, very rich loam, it is a heavy feeder that soon exhausts normal garden soil; many cultivated varieties known

THE vetchling in the plate was first described as a Sicilian wild flower in a published work of 1697 by a priest-botanist, Fr. Cupani. It was unusual in the genus in that it had a fragrance. By 1700 it was being grown by Dr Robert Uvedale, a noted English headmaster, botanist, and gardener, who was one of the first to make extensive use of greenhouses and guessed intuitively the needs of imported exotics. A contemporary reported: *'His greens take up six or seven houses . . . His flowers are choice, his stock numerous, and his culture of them very methodical and curious.'* Until gout seized him in his eightieth year, the Doctor ran his school and his gardens and made botanical collections. If he is remembered for nothing else, he deserves fame as the first to introduce into cultivation the progenitor of a massive and illustrious family of hardy climbers, the Sweet Pea.

It has been claimed that *L. odoratus* has grown itself out and disappeared from its original home; even that the few in cultivation in the Old World have been brought back from Ecuador in the New where the plant was established when that country was part of the Viceroyalty of Peru. Nevertheless plants can still be found growing in limestone in the protection of woody places in southern Italy that bear so strong a resemblance they may surely be counted as descendants. Their other, more showy collaterals owe most to an English florist, Henry Eckford, who began to cross Sweet Peas in 1870. At that date it was customary to make up mixed bunches of the flowers. Soon, as he developed different strains, bunches were made of distinct colours. His extraordinary successes were further improved, and nurserymen are still working to find a true yellow or true blue variety which has so far eluded them.

The heyday of the Sweet Pea was in 1900 when the bicentenary of its introduction was celebrated by an exhibition and a conference at the London Crystal Palace, but the glorious strains of that era such as Apple Blossom, Emily Eckford, Venus, Duke of Clarence, Stanley, and Ignea have long disappeared, and given way to literally thousands of named cultivars of different types, size, and shades of colour. The invariable factor is their scent. A garden catalogue of 1772 attempted to describe it: *'Somewhat like Honey and a little tending to the Orange-flower Smell.'* It was close, but not close enough. No one has ever quite managed to conjure up in words that matchless scent.

Plate 42

Lathyrus odoratus

Tragopogon hybridus L.

GOAT'S-BEARD, SMOOTH GEROPOGON

FAMILY: Compositae
SYNONYM: *Geropogon glaber* L.
DISTRIBUTION: Mediterranean region and southern Europe
CULTIVATION: hardy annual; prefers well-drained soil and plenty of light

EXACT identification from a plate engraved in 1800 is not easy. The *Botanical Magazine* issued this figure under Linnaeus's generic name of *Geropogon* from the Greek for old man and beard. Later he changed his mind and concocted *Tragopogon*, meaning Goat's-beard. He also conducted an experiment, deliberately crossing two of its species, the red-purple Salsify and the common yellow Goat's-beard. This was in 1759 and was historically important as the first instance of a man-made plant 'marriage' being recorded scientifically.

But, just as probably, the plate illustrates the Italian Goat's-beard, *T. crocifolium*, that had long been established as a garden flower. In England it was cultivated by Mary, Duchess of Beaufort, a lady cruelly caught up in the English Civil War and the Glorious Revolution, who suffered much from an erratic husband, lost two sons, and took consolation in horticulture. And it is certain she was growing the plant before 1704 as that was the publication date of John Ray's *Historia Plantarum* in which it was first listed.

Much has always been made of the English herbalists Turner, Gerard, and Parkinson, even of that unlikeable charlatan Culpeper, but John Ray has never achieved equal fame. Yet from his published works it is arguable that he ranks next to Darwin amongst English naturalists. He was a blacksmith's son and scholarships took him to Cambridge where he was ordained priest and became a Fellow of Trinity. He lost this security when, as a matter of conscience over religious issues, he had to leave the University. Thereafter he travelled widely, working as a field naturalist in places as far apart as Malta and the Isle of Man, generally accompanied by a close friend. When, quite unexpectedly, his friend died, Ray had no heart to travel any more. He returned to his native village, married, fathered four daughters, and lived as a scholarly recluse remote from the dramatic political struggles of the day. He was too poor to have his books illustrated. Moreover, he would not chase the popular hares of astrology and quackery, and he wrote in Latin. Therefore he was never given recognition in England and he died, sadly and in great pain from ulceration, not long after he listed and described the graceful Italian Goat's-beard as a garden plant in cultivation. On the Continent, where Latin was still the lingua franca,[1] his work was highly regarded and sought after.

[1] Latin remained the official language of the Austro-Hungarian Empire until 1848.

90

Plate 43

Tragopogon hybridus

Typhonium roxburghii Schott

THREE-LOBED ARUM

FAMILY: Araceae
SYNONYMS: *Arum trilobatum* Roxb., *Arisarum amboinense* Rumph.
DISTRIBUTION: Sri Lanka, Malaysia, and Indonesia
CULTIVATION: perennial herb for stove culture; prefers some shade; propagated by
corm offsets

A tropical *Typhonium* attracts pollinating flies by its smell. To some it suggests rotting compost, to others boiling meat, and a few find it unbearable. But it is not pervasive, its intensity depending on the state of the plant's development and the atmosphere in which it grows. To those who are insensitive or indifferent to its odour, this little species *T. roxburghii*, apparently a miniature Arum but botanically in a different genus, is an interesting subject for the hothouse. Its most noticeable feature is the length of its spadix in proportion to the spathe and the leaves. The lower part of this tapering club is pocked and pitted. The plate is well done. It is useful to see it has a tuberous root with fleshy threads and it shows clearly the colour combination of brown and murrey and royal purple and differing shades of green with the striking marbling and freckling. Yet it cannot quite indicate the texture of a living plant, part velvet, part metallic in sheen.

The species was anonymously introduced into cultivation in Europe before 1714 when we know it was being grown by a London nurseryman. The first to write it up was Georg Everhard Rumpf who was Deputy Governor of Amboina in the Spice Islands from 1657 until he died in 1702. Though this claw-shaped little island was first discovered and claimed by the Portuguese in 1562 and was always part of the native Kingdom of Tidor, it was a bone of contention between the Dutch and the British for more than a hundred years. Britain twice seized and held it for short periods. But this was long after Meinheer Rumpf had found *T. roxburghii* growing there, and given the warning that the roots contained a poison which caused '*violent inflammation of the mouth and throat*' if eaten raw by mistake. It suggests first- or second-hand experience which is not to be wondered at in view of Rumpf's wretched history. The poor man wrote an immense *Herbarium Amboinense* dealing with about 1,200 species but it never got into print until forty years after his death, and this was the least of the disasters that plagued him. A fire wiped out almost all his collections and drawings; he lost his sight; and his home was destroyed and his wife and daughter killed in a violent earthquake.

Plate 44

Typhonium roxburghii

Aloe variegata L.

PARTRIDGE-BREASTED ALOE, TIGER ALOE

FAMILY: Liliaceae
DISTRIBUTION: South Africa, in the dry Karoo regions
CULTIVATION: non-hardy perennial; needs warm dry conditions with plenty of light, it can be kept as a house-plant; propagation by suckers, leaf-cuttings, or by seed

ALOES have been cultivated for centuries as the source of the valuable drug aloes. The leaves are triangular in section and when sliced from the parent they ooze quantities of yellow sap. Commercially this is collected, rendered by heat, and left to solidify before being used for a variety of purposes. Generations of finger-biting children have been familiar with the unpleasant, stringent taste. And Aloes have long been valued as an exotic foliage plant though the species figured, *A. variegata*, was late to cross the equator from the Cape of Good Hope. Other Cape species, amongst them the peculiar Fan Aloe that grows higher than a man, throwing out branches to make a bush, were well established before the aptly named Partridge-breasted Aloe was introduced into cultivation about 1720. It was to outrival all other Aloes as a manageable pot plant for summering out of doors. Its closest rival, the Tree Aloe, has, as its name suggests, the disadvantage of growing to 3 metres (8 feet) and more. In the varieties found in and near the Cape there are five kinds of Aloe: climbing, large, medium, small, and miniature. *A. variegata* is a miniature; its tuft of keeled, speckled leaves scarcely reaching 13 centimetres (6 inches); its spike of coral red flowers that hold a pearl drop of nectar scarcely ever span 30 centimetres (a foot). Furthermore, its Cape name Kanniedood means 'Cannot Die' and indicates its hardiness. As a house-plant it can be mistreated by allowing the leaves to sit on damp soil instead of a bed of pebbles and it can be murdered by allowing water to settle in the rosette of leaves. At the Cape it can stand frost to some extent, and any amount of heat. In fact the more sun the plant has, the richer will be the colouring of its warty, stringy foliage. A protective second skin or cuticle allows the plant to take in water very easily and lose it by evaporation very slowly. For this reason it can withstand lengthy drought. A torn-off shrivelled leaf will plump up rapidly if soaked in water. A whole plant uprooted and left on the ground for a long period will still come to life again on replanting. An interesting and accommodating succulent.

Plate 45

Aloe variegata

Trichosanthes anguina L.

SNAKE-GOURD, VIPER-GOURD, SERPENT CUCUMBER

FAMILY: cucurbitaceae
DISTRIBUTION: Indo-Malaysia, Australia, and China
CULTIVATION: half-hardy annual; if ripe fruits are required it is better grown in a
greenhouse

THE Snake-gourd or Serpent Cucumber originated in the Far East where it has a long history of utility to man. It was not, though, introduced to the West until the 1720s when the Italian Abbot, Josephus Ignatius Cordero, took seeds from China to his native Tuscany that were grown successfully in the Pisa Botanic Garden. Thirty years later consignments of seeds were sent direct from China to Sir Hans Sloane's Physic Garden in Chelsea which he had made over to the Company of Apothecaries. The garden superintendent, Philip Miller, famous internationally for his *Gardener's Dictionary*, was considered 'an ingenious florist' well able to coax difficult subjects into growth and he had no trouble in bringing the Snake-gourd into flower and fruit in the Chelsea stove. For some reason or other seeds were not introduced to France until 1804, the year it was figured in the February issue of the *Botanical Magazine*. It was slow therefore to enter general cultivation, and even today it is not often seen growing in the West. In view of its qualities this seems strange.

Even amongst so many lovely coloured engravings this plate is exceptional for its exactness and for the beauty of the design. Because of the fretted or laced edge to the white flower Linnaeus gave the gourd its generic name from *trichos*, meaning hair, and anthos, flower, though a grosser image suggests the frilly flower is more like the irregularly meshed net of membrane from a pig's alimentary canal, sometimes called its skirt. The fruit shown in the plate is young. As it ripens it becomes buttercup yellow. But, like all other plates, even this has limitations. It cannot convey the smell of the Snake-gourd flower which most closely resembles a combination of cake icing and hot metal, with just a suggestion of raw meat. Nor can it indicate the size of the plant or its phenomenal rate of growth. Well watered and nourished, it can grow 3.6 metres (12 feet) in six weeks and is valued in the East because it so quickly makes shade. It is also a delicious vegetable and, if left to dry, the hard outer skin makes a useful container. Finally, an American evaluation of the economic plants of China gives it a good rating. The Snake-gourd is excellent fodder for hogs.

Plate 46

Trichosanthes anguina

Reseda odorata L.

SWEET-SCENTED RESEDA, MIGNONETTE

FAMILY: resedaceae
DISTRIBUTION: mountains of North Africa (Cyrenaica)
CULTIVATION: hardy annual or perennial; prefers rich loamy soil, grows well in half shade

MIGNONETTE has a long history. It was used as a fragrant herb in the elaborate funeral ceremonies of Pharaonic Egypt. Then Pliny tells us it was used by the doctors of his day for reducing tumours. They would lay the plant on the swelling and utter the charm *Reseda morbis*. This was the imperative of an extremely rare Latin verb *resedare*, to assuage or heal. Thus Pliny gave the plant its generic name. Despite its ancient utilities, and despite its sweet scent and the attraction of its greenish-white flowers that gave its name to mignonette green in the colour dictionary, *R. odorata* was not cultivated until 1725 when the French began to appreciate it. Like the Germans they used and still use the plant's generic name, calling it *réséda*. Philip Miller, who first grew it in England, listed it in his *Gardener's Dictionary* as Bastard Rocket (commonly called Sweet Reseda), or Mignonette d'Egypt, and commended its *'high ambrosial scent'*. It slowly became a general favourite until, like a work of literature that does not begin to sell until long, long after publication, it suddenly became highly fashionable and everyone was growing it. The impetus was given by no less a person than Napoleon who found time on his Egyptian campaign to send seeds of *réséda* from its native home to the Empress Josephine. She being an enthusiastic if temperamental gardener set the mode of growing it as a pot plant and it became the rage in conservatories, window boxes, and as a house-plant. Being so strongly scented it had an obvious attraction during a period when rooms were overcrammed with furniture and airless and stuffy, and city streets offensive. Not only was it the most popular pot plant but for years it was used in bouquets especially during the winter when the gardeners of the Riveria made fortunes out. of forced flowers. It was created as an annual until a 'Tree Mignonette' turned up in Liège. This was considered a separate species until it was discovered that, by growing the plant under glass and pinching out flowers, it becomes what one Victorian devotee called *'a gigantic wonder'*. The truly extraordinary thing is that, in the last quarter of the twentieth century and in an era when house-plants have never been sold and written about so much, the Mignonette is unobtainable and only mentioned by a few sapient specialists. Ichabod.

Plate 47

Reseda odorata

Catesbaea spinosa L.

THORNY CATESBAEA, LILY THORN

FAMILY: Rubiaceae
DISTRIBUTION: Bahama Islands
CULTIVATION: non-hardy shrub up to 5 metres (15 feet) tall; better planted in a warm greenhouse but it can be placed out of doors in summer; propagated by seed or by cuttings

EAST Anglia has nursed many of the greatest British naturalists. John Catesby was born and brought up there, being acquainted with the modest genius John Ray, and though he went twice to the colonies, first as the guest of his brother-in-law who was Secretary of State in Virginia, and then sponsored by a number of fellow British naturalists *'with the professed design of describing, delineating and painting the more curious objects of nature'*, he was only out of England for eleven of his seventy years. On such short acquaintance it is remarkable that the United States should claim him as a leading American scientist, and that he was able to produce such a massively comprehensive work as *The Natural History of Carolina, Florida[1] and the Bahama Islands*, as well as send so many living and dried plants to his friends and patrons in England. Etching was an expensive business and so Catesby decided to learn how to do it for himself. He took lessons and etched and hand-coloured all but two of the 222 plates that illustrated his work. They were unusual because they ranged widely over natural history subjects and he included birds and fish and insects in the same plate, after the style of Madame Merian before him and John Audubon after him. Birds greatly interested Catesby and he had ornithological views far in advance of his time.[2] A strange facet of 18th century publishing is revealed by the fact that a rich friend pensioned him so that he could print and sell his own work and make a little money out of it *'else through necessity it must have fallen a prey to the bookseller'*. Linnaeus honoured Catesby by naming after him a genus of evergreen shrubs. The species figured here was found by Catesby himself when he was living for a time on the Island of Providence in the Bahamas. Called the Thorn Lily in English it can grow to 3 metres (9 feet) high so the plate must illustrate a young bush flowering precociously. It is almost a pre-Raphaelite study in frog yellow and green of prickles, bold leaves, and pendulous trumpet flowers.

[1] The 'Florida' of his title was soon to be called 'Georgia'.
[2] In a paper he read to the Royal Society on being made a Fellow, Catesby scorned the theory that swallows hibernated in ponds and said temperatures and food supplies were at the back of migration.

Plate 48

Catesbaea spinosa

Cornus florida L.

GREAT-FLOWERED CORNEL, FLOWERING DOGWOOD

FAMILY: Cornaceae
SYNONYM: *Cynoxylon floridum* L.
DISTRIBUTION: U.S.A. from Maine to Florida
CULTIVATION: tree up to 10 metres (30 feet) tall or it can be kept as a branched shrub,
generally hardy but somewhat susceptible to late frosts; prefers a moist soil; propagated
by seed

THE Dogwoods of Europe, though reputedly useful as the sources of lamp-oil, butchers' wooden skewers, fresh and pickled fruit, and a preserve, and with decorative bark in springtime and fruit and leaves in autumn, can scarcely compare for beauty with the North American species. Therefore it is unfortunate that, though perfectly hardy and still growing in many European countries, they have never fully adapted themselves to the Old World and do better in the New.

The first to be found and introduced to Europe from the early settlements was *C. florida*, called Flowering Dogwood. It was grown in 1730 and later distributed by the nurseryman Thomas Fairchild about whom little is known save that he was acquainted with eminent botanists – an interest in plants being as potent an equalizer as music, painting, and sculpture – and that he was responsible for introducing quite a number of exotics into Europe. He was one of the more successful commercial growers who had gardens in parts of the country near London which, on account of the needs of a growing population, have since been obliterated. It is an odd thought that *Typhonium roxburghii, Aloe variegata, Catesbaea spinosa* as well as *Cornus florida*, all selected for inclusion in this volume, were first cultivated in Fairchild's nursery at Hoxton that afterwards became an insalubrious slum.

The Flowering Dogwood is a perfectly adequate name for those who grow this tree and enjoy looking at it, but the name irritates purists. Actually the flowers are insignificant, being crowded together in a green and yellow little blob at the centre of the four or sometimes more chalk-white bracts that resemble petals. These are attractive, as the plate well shows, but perhaps the plant is at its best in autumn when the bracts form to enclose the flowerhead until spring. Simultaneously the red-berried fruit of the previous season's growth is being consumed by the North American Mocking Bird or Hundred-tongued Bird, and the oval opposite leaves, which have been dark green above and a softer green below, turn a vivid rusty phoeniceous colour and stand like flames until a high wind or a hard frost brings them down.

Plate 49

Cornus florida

Petrea racemosa Nees

TWINING PETREA, PURPLE WREATH

FAMILY: Verbenaceae
SYNONYM: *Petrea volubilis* auct. non L.
DISTRIBUTION: Central America and West Indies
CULTIVATION: perennial climber for the warm greenhouse; it takes a long time to
become established but, given enough light, it will bloom profusely when established;
propagated by cuttings which often take a long time to root

THE artistically designed plate shows one of the most opulent climbers, known as Queen's Wreath in its native West Indies, as Sandpaper Vine on the mainland nearby, and often as Purple Wreath in the Old World. Its hairy flowers are variable in colour, from navy-blue to lilac that fade to a smoky grey, and the hanging racemes are anything up to 30 centimetres (a foot) long. It is a twiner that, fed well and kept warm, will scramble up to 6.5 metres (20 feet) and more, or it can be cut back and clipped to make a shrub. The leaves are leathery, 20 centimetres (8 inches) long by 7.5 centimetres (3 inches) wide, and a beryl-green. If the climate permits and the plant is allowed to twine its way over a host with different foliage, say an old unfruitful olive, the contrast is very effective.

The Purple Wreath's botanic name honours a young nobleman of East Anglia, Robert, Lord Petre, who, at the age of 16, joined a syndicate of naturalists engaged to hire a plant-hunter for £200 a year to '*improve botany in Georgia*'. He was also required to send back new plants and seeds for which purpose he was allowed to roam at will in the south-eastern parts of the colonies, Mexico, and the West Indies. They chose a Scot who thus became the first in a line of professional Scotch botanical explorers so long that it stretched far into the twentieth century. William Houston had already been to the West Indies and was an experienced traveller. He had also read medicine for two years at Leyden and graduated, earning something of a name for his work on respiration. He was admitted Fellow of the Royal Society but lacked funds and was glad to make an agreement. He left for Georgia in 1729 at the age of 34 presumably taking with him a consignment of plants for the colony's improvement. In the following four years he travelled widely, sending seeds and plants to the Chelsea Physic Garden. Among them was a species of *Dorstenia* that by repute cured snake bites and which is remarkable among plants in the way in which the fruit receptacle swells, puts pressure on the fruit, and jerks it out like a slippery pip popped from between two fingers. In 1733 when in Vera Cruz Houston found the Purple Wreath climber and named it for Lord Petre who was still only 20. Then he went on to Jamaica where, despite his experience as a traveller and despite his particular knowledge of respiration, he dropped dead from the heat in the middle of August.

Plate 50

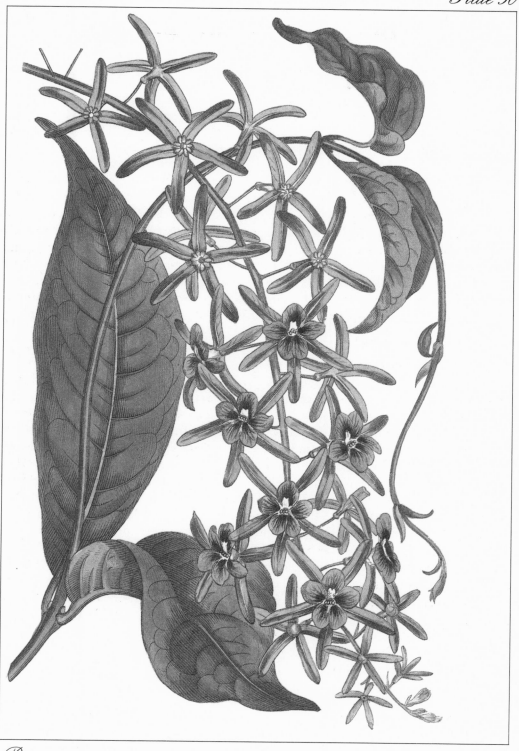

Petrea racemosa

Gordonia lasianthus (L.) Ellis

LOBLOLLY BAY, BLACK LAUREL

FAMILY: Theaceae
DISTRIBUTION: south-eastern U.S.A. from Virginia to Florida
CULTIVATION: evergreen tree or shrub; needs moist acid soil and protection in winter;
propagated by seed or by cuttings

ROBERT, Lord Petre, had his name immortalized in the climber figured in the preceding plate. His head gardener, James Gordon, was immortalized in the ornamental tree figured here, first introduced from North America and grown in Chelsea at some time before 1739.

Gordon was enterprising. When his master died at the early age of 29, he went up to London and established not only a nursery in the nearby countryside but also a seed shop right in the heart of the city. He was a noted propagator, able to manage the tiny dusty seeds of some plants that generally defeated gardeners and strike cuttings where others failed. As a result he made not only a name but a great deal of money as a supplier to fellow nurserymen. For example, by propagating from four original cuttings of a species of Gardenia he made £500 in less than three years, a fortune at that period. Ironically he was less successful with the Loblolly Bay that was named after him. He recognised its potential for, as a white-flowered evergreen, it was only marginally inferior to the Magnolia and its bark was used in tanning. As soon as he opened his nursery in 1743 he began trials with the intention of propagating it on a commercial scale. But the Loblolly was a difficult subject, by no means as hardy in the European temperate zone as in its native home on the south-eastern seaboard of North America. It took Gordon twenty years of patient experiment before he successfully grew the tree from seed and founded a valuable colony of stock. In 1758 he was commended to Linnaeus as *'having more knowledge in vegetation than all the gardeners and writers on gardening in England put together'*. This was, perhaps, overwarm praise for though Dr Uvedale was dead, Philip Miller still reigned at Chelsea. However, thenceforth the great systematist corresponded with the Mile End nurseryman.

The Loblolly belongs to the distinguished order of Tea plants, *Theaceae*, that includes Camellias and Stewartias. Whence its English name derives is uncertain. Loblolly is an old seaman's word for gruel, maybe because porridge in the pot makes a loblolly, guggling noise. At sea it gave rise to loblolly boy, the surgeon's mate. On shore, weirdly, and for no apparent reason, it was attached both to a pine and to *Gordonia lasianthus*.

Plate 51

Gordonia lasianthus

Dodecatheon meadia L.

SHOOTING STARS, MEAD'S DODECATHEON

FAMILY: Primulaceae
DISTRIBUTION: Atlantic North America
CULTIVATION: hardy perennial; prefers sandy soil, wet in winter but dry in summer
and a sunny position; propagation by seed or by root cuttings (other species can be
propagated by division of the rhizome)

SHOOTING STARS, as the Americans descriptively name this genus, is principally confined to the east coast of their continent. It was twice introduced to Europe. On the first occasion seeds were sent late in the 17th century by the clergyman-naturalist John Baptist Banister, a martyr to botany for, according to one version, he was shot while collecting and, according to another, he fell a great height and broke his neck. The seeds were sent to his Bishop, Henry Compton, for not only were all Crown dependencies then considered as a part of the Diocese of London, but the Bishop was a famous plantsman. The pleasure grounds of his palace were virtually a botanic garden and there Shooting Stars were sown and grown. Then either the plant disappeared or stocks in cultivation were so low that it became a variety known to very few. A second introduction took place in about 1745. It was successful and Mark Catesby, in his flora of the early colonies, gave it the generic name *Meadia* after a fashionable London physician who practised medicine partly in his own home but chiefly in a city coffee house. Linnaeus considered it a misplaced honour. Dr Mead might be physician to the King of England, the Prime Minister, Sir Isaac Newton, and the poet Pope, but botanically he was entirely undistinguished. In an unusual burst of irritation the Great Systematist arbitrarily used Dr Mead's name only for this species and the genus he renamed *Dodecatheon*, from the Greek for twelve gods, a figure suggested by the average number of its 'stars'.

At that period the flower was greatly popular in England. It was figured in one of the most fascinating flower books ever published, Dr Thornton's *Temple of Flora*, and Dr Erasmus Darwin, grandfather of the author of *Origin of Species* and poet of some remarkably awful floral verses, was moved to describe the five turned-back mauve petals and the prominent stamens, in a quatrain of careful observations:

> *Meadia's soft chain five suppliant beaux confess,*
> *And hand in hand the laughing belle address;*
> *Alike to all she bows with wanton air,*
> *Rolls her dark eyes, and waves her golden hair.*

In the wild state Shooting Stars are found on dry sandy hillsides, marshes, and open woods, and range in colour from deep pink to lavender. Cultivated plants grow larger, up to 60 centimetres (2 feet) in height.

Plate 52

Dodecatheon meadia

Watsonia meriana (L.) Miller

WATSONIA

FAMILY: Iridaceae
SYNONYM: *Antholyza meriana* L.
DISTRIBUTION: South Africa
CULTIVATION: non-hardy corm that prefers a well-drained, sunny position, it is better cultivated under glass but can be planted outdoors during the summer; propagated by corm offsets or by seed

BEING conspicuously coloured natives of South Africa and having the same sword-like leaves, some species of *Watsonia* are confused with *Gladiolus*. An easy test distinguishes them. Examine the pistil. If it is divided into three it is a *Gladiolus*. If it is divided into six it is a *Watsonia*.

W. meriana was one of the very first to be brought to Europe from the Cape about the middle of the 18th century. It grows to a height of between 100 and 130 centimetres (3 and 4 feet), but there is a small form of the species of 22.5 centimetres (9 inches) that is frequently confused with *W. humilis* introduced in 1754. In the Cape it is called Lakpypie, and, refusing to adapt itself to another hemisphere, north of the equator it flowers in spring and early summer. Specialist growers warn laymen of the difficulty of telling one species from another; firstly, because they are concupiscent crossers and, given the opportunity, turn out any number of hybrids; and secondly, because save for the pure white species, there are frequent colour variations in every shade of mauve, orange, red, and pink. This is more than borne out by the plate which figures a plant three-quarters through its blooming, the buds and flower trumpets a glittering display of brick red, salmon pink, liver, magenta, indigo blue, and violet. It provokes the frequently posed question of whether or not colours can clash in nature. There are those who say they can and do; that a mineral like Indian jasper is a petrified example, and a Streaked Gurnard and the underside wings of a male Two-tailed Pasha are living ones. The majority deny it and claim that only the highest form of creation is capable of clashing colours. Flower arrangers will be shy of such a garish plant, though in South Africa Lakpypies are frequently used as a cut flower, the stems being burnt as soon as they are cut.

Philip Miller grew the species from seed at Chelsea and named the genus *Watsonia* for Sir William Watson, an ornament of 18th century science, an expert in electrical gadgetry, insulation, inoculation, famed internationally for his paper on the Star Puff-ball, and described as '*a living lexicon of botany*'. The German botanist Dr Trew of Nuremburg named it *meriana* to honour the Dutch lady Madame Merian who, before 1700, courageously went to South America to draw insects with great dash and some inaccuracy and whose zeal carried her a rather special title in what was then very much a man's world. She was called '*a female votary of the sciences*'.

Plate 53

Watsonia meriana

Sarracenia flava L.

YELLOW SIDE-SADDLE FLOWER, YELLOW SARRACENIA

FAMILY: Sarraceniaceae
DISTRIBUTION: south-eastern U.S.A., from Virginia to Florida
CULTIVATION: hardy perennial somewhat sensitive to late frosts; requires moist but not wet acid conditions and is easily grown in peat mixed with sand, in summer it needs partial shade; propagated by seed or by careful division of the rootstock

THE flowers of this North American bog plant are singular. Its style exactly resembles a green trap umbrella and between the spokes hang the yellow petals. The early European settlers saw a different resemblance. In the days of elegance, before women took to breeches, they hooked their right leg over the pummel of the saddle in much the same way as the petal hangs over the expanded style of this plant. Thus it was named the Side-saddle Flower. They are long lasting, remaining in character for several weeks. But the flowers are even less singular than the leaves that grow from a rosette and are hollow jug-shaped vessels and pit-fall traps for insects. The lip of the entrance is like a lobster-pot, involuted and designed to allow an insect to enter but not to emerge. The insect is attracted by honey-glands, becomes bemused or lulled by the sweetness, and hurtles down what botanists term 'the slide-zone' into a broth of digestive liquid rich with decomposing bodies. If it tries to get away by scrambling up the tube it meets a mass of downward-pointing hairs that are impassable. So the Side-saddle Flower is a carnivorous plant and an object of fascination especially to those with the imagination to visualize the plant enjoying insect banquets with the relish of an ogre crunching up his victims. Nevertheless carnivorous plants are not merely a Divine caprice. Bogland is short of soluble nitrates and Side-saddle Flowers are able to make up for this deficiency by assimilating nitrogen from the corpses drowned in their ingeniously constructed leaves.

A purple species of *Sarracenia* was first sent to Europe by a Dr Sarrazin of Quebec for whom the genus is named, and it was in cultivation by 1640. More than a century passed before *S. flava* was being grown in the chelsea Physic Garden in 1752. And even in 1804, when this plate was published, the purpose of the peculiar leaves was still unknown. There was a vague notion that the insect-polluted water might in some way be serviceable, an idea indicated by some of the names also used for the plant in North America – Forefather's Cup, Huntsman's Cup, Indian Cup, and Soldier's Drinking Cup.

Plate 54

Sarracenia flava

Hypoxis stellata L. var. *Gawleri* Baker

YELLOW STAR-HYPOXIS

FAMILY: Hypoxidaceae
DISTRIBUTION: South Africa
CULTIVATION: non-hardy corm that should be kept in a cool greenhouse, resting corms must be kept dry; propagated by corm offsets or by seed

THIS handsome Cape plant was being grown in the Chelsea Physic Garden in 1752. By an extraordinary coincidence, and in ample demonstration of the wide distribution of the genus, a North American species was also being grown there at that very same time. Both had yellow and starry flowers but the North American was hairy and less showy and smaller than its cousin from the Cape of Good Hope.

H. stellata var. *gawleri*, called Midday Stars in South Africa on account of its habit of opening only in the sun, is without any perceptible scent, and it has a number of colour variations. The brightest has flowers of light pink or ivory or chalk white marked with a violet patch and a sea-green eye, and the special name Peacock Stars. The flower figured here is less bright but still striking. There are yet others, entirely yellow without markings, and some in drearier shades of straw and bronze and khaki, all marked with a livid brown. There are also some variations in size, between 15 and 33 centimetres (6 and 12 inches).

The plant grows from a rhizome or corm encased in a netting of membrane that easily rots if over-watered during its resting period. The broad leaves are a fresh green and flabby, and well set off the sharply defined flowers. They have a fibrous edge that can be felt between the fingers and, as they twist in spirals, they taper to limp mousetails.

It is not known who first carried the plant northwards on the inward-bound passage but it was quickly written up by several distinguished European botanists and roused the interest and admiration of gardeners. Yet, though it makes modest demands as to soil and food, and only requires baking in sun and cautious use of the watering pot, the plant was never widely grown and only recently have some discriminating seedsmen begun to include it in their catalogues.

Plate 55

Hypoxis stellata

Crinum bulbispermum (Burm.) Milne-Redh. & Schweik.

LONG-LEAVED CRINUM

FAMILY: Amaryllidaceae
SYNONYM: *Amaryllis longiflora* L.
DISTRIBUTION: South Africa
CULTIVATION: half-hardy bulb but some races and hybrids are fully hardy; needs a lot of water during the growing period; propagated by bulb offsets or by seed

THERE are certain tricks used in botanical illustration. By leaving out five flowers, the two shown in the plate and the huge leaf left incomplete at each end, the artist gives the impression this *Crinum* species is very large. It is, and in full bloom it requires staking. The bulb is in proportion, and the size and shape of a footlight bulb. The dozen or so leaves are a glossy green, 7.5 centimetres (3 inches) wide and a metre (3 feet) long. The stalk grows to between 30 centimetres and a metre (1 and 3 feet), and from the onion-skin spathe that crowns it each fragrant flower has a 7.5 centimetre (3 inch) stalk. The original species, brought from the Cape in the first half of the 18th century, had between six and twelve flowers. Under modern gardening conditions they manage to produce about twenty that open in succession. But in fact the species is seldom grown nowadays, having been 'improved' by a Californian hybridist who crossed it with an established hybrid and evolved Cape Dawn, a massive and marvellous plant, 1.6 metres (5 feet) tall with flesh-coloured flowers.

Like so many other exotics in the Golden Age of Botany, this *Crinum* was cultivated and written up by Philip Miller who was the first to grow many of the plants figured in this selection of plates. He was a Scot who managed the Chelsea Physic Garden for the Company of Apothecaries for forty-eight years and was internationally renowned for his *Gardener's Dictionary* that ran through eight editions in his own lifetime. There was no doubting his green fingers at a time when horticulture was groping in the dark, nor his initiative[1] and shrewdness. Never too proud to pick up good ideas, he was secretary of a group of experts who met regularly to exchange their gardening skills, but, doubtless for temperamental reasons, the group '*broke up rather abruptly*'. Miller was asked to return all papers containing information to their owners, which he did expeditiously – having the foresight to take a copy of each beforehand. He was elected a Fellow of the Royal Society and was much praised by Linnaeus, who gave him a packet of dried South American plants and became his correspondent. But he was dour and obstinate and, for some unknown reason, he was pensioned off at the good age of 79. However, he is not yet forgotten by gardeners.

[1] He used the bowls of clay pipes and old lobster claws as earwig traps.

Plate 56

Crinum bulbispermum

Hypericum chinense L.

CHINESE ST. JOHN'S WORT

FAMILY: Guttiferae
SYNONYM: *Hypericum monogynum* L.
DISTRIBUTION: China and Japan
CULTIVATION: half-hardy shrub; better kept in a cool greenhouse; propagated by seed
or by cuttings

THE Chinese St. John's Wort is unusual in that it is an evergreen that occasionally sheds its leaves. Not surprisingly some gardeners are alarmed by this sudden, yet quite healthy baldness, mistakenly considering it a sign of incipient death. It is also unusual in that it sometimes has a single terminal flower and sometimes a flattish pyramidal head of up to seven flowers called a cyme. Most St. John's Worts are consistent and have either one or the other. Finally the Chinese species has a much longer flowering period than most others and, if it is kept in a cool house, it will be in bloom for the greater part of the year.

The beauty of the flower is an aesthetic bonus as it serves no obvious practical purpose to the plant. It has no stores of honey, and no attractive fragrance because each flower is fertilized either by its own abundant pollen or by pollen from a neighbouring flower in the same cyme. This accounts for the number of upstanding stamens. On the rare occasions when the stigma is longer than the stamens there is a chance that wind-borne pollen from another species will get there first, and so produce a hybrid, but this is an irregularity in the life-cycle of the hermaphrodite St. John's Wort.

The species was introduced from China into European gardens in 1753 by the then Duke of Northumberland, English Vice-admiral of all America who took refuge from his 'junketaceous' Duchess in statecraft, scholarship, and in the arms of a very rich cousin who produced a bastard called James Louis or Louis Macie Smithson. The fruit of this irregularity in the Duke's life showed a repugnance for his parents' country and he lived chiefly and in some splendour in Paris, Berlin, Rome, and Florence, but he shared his father's interest in natural science and, on his death in Genoa, he left his huge fortune to the United States, then a baby nation, for the founding of the Smithsonian Institute in Washington.

Plate 57

Hypericum chinense

Erinacea anthyllis Link

HEDGEHOG BROOM, BRANCH THORN

FAMILY: Leguminosae
SYNONYMS: *Anthyllis erinacea* L., *Erinacea pungens* Boiss.
DISTRIBUTION: calcareous mountains of the western Mediterranean region
CULTIVATION: dwarf shrub, some races are hardy, others need protection in winter; prefers a well-drained, limey soil; propagated by seed or by layering

IN his long and careworn life the Flemish botanist Clusius enjoyed few cloudless days. Possibly the brightest were on a plant-hunting expedition he made with two pupils through Spain and Portugal in 1564. Even then he met with accidents, damaging on one occasion a leg, and, on another, falling down a precipice on his horse, breaking his botanizing right arm. Nevertheless he had the anodyne of discovering over 200 new species of plants, one of which was the prickly shrub figured in the plate.

The writer of the original letterpress in the *Botanical Magazine* was unusually enthusiastic: '*The finding of his little beauty, armed at all points against his invading gripe, whilst it deferred his possession, must have prolonged his pleasure, and added to the value of his prize; well might he exultingly style it "plane nova et tota elegans".*' Appositely Clusius named the plant *Erinacea* after the Latin and Spanish for a hedgehog, and in English it is called Hedgehog Broom or Branch Thorn. But Clusius found no seed and for a long time succeeding botanists were no more fortunate. The Hedgehog Broom is a slow grower and it takes some time to establish as a domed shrub the size of a pail. It is also slow to flower. It is only speedy in shedding its small leaves.

There is no record of it being in cultivation before 1759, almost two hundred years after its discovery. This is possibly because, like other less hardy shrubs, it failed to become established until the science of greenhousing was sufficiently advanced. Once accepted by gardeners it was valued for its compactness, its unusual blue flowers, and its prickly evergreen branches that are silky and hairy when young.

In common with many other botanical finds this bristly bush has passed through the fire of numerous namings. Caspar Bauhin wrote it up in 1623 and, although it had a longer calyx of sepals than most species of *Genista*, he put it in that genus. Then in 1753 Linnaeus decided it was probably a species of *Anthyllis* although its simple, lower leaves are arranged opposite to one another. His name, *Anthyllis erinacea*, was accepted from 1753 until 1831 when Johann Link, founder of the Berlin herbarium, restored Clusius's name and, for good measure, used Linnaeus's name as a specific. Thus it ended up as *E. anthyllis*.

Plate 58

Erinacea anthyllis

Hemerocallis minor Miller

NARROW-LEAVED DAY LILY

FAMILY: Liliaceae
SYNONYM: *Hemerocallis graminea* Andr.
DISTRIBUTION: eastern Asia
CULTIVATION: hardy perennial; very adaptable but enjoys a sunny position;
propagated by dividing the rootstock

So many plants are used for food in the East that the Western list of cultivated vegetables is puny, almost austere. Species of *Hemerocallis* are highly esteemed as *gum jum*, golden needles, and *gum tsoy*, golden vegetables, and added to many dishes. In the West we chiefly use them for that unadventurous thing 'the easy garden' as they will grow in virtually any soil and bloom in the tropics as well as close to the Arctic Circle. They are planted in clumps and require no attention for some time. They should not, however, be grown too close to a pasture as a cow, wiser in her tastes than we are, will go to great lengths to get at the succulent leaves.

Hemerocallis is named for the Greek words for day and beauty because their flowers are ephemeral and do not survive twenty-four hours. As they have many flowers in succession and handsome foliage this is not a major fault. The genus has about twenty species and most have their homeland in Japan though, by the hand of man, they have been spread over the face of the earth, and again, by the hand of man, cultivars have been developed which make nonsense of their name, Day Lily, because some named varieties last for two or three.

The two flower specimens in the plate are from two distinct plants, the lower being grown from seeds sent from east Siberia, the upper from descendants of plants grown in England since the days of Parkinson. Regrettably, they are at different stages of maturity, and the leaf, which is grass-like and a fairly sound indication of the species, does not appear to be associated with either. It would also be helpful to know if the roots of each plant are slender and fibrous or thick and fleshy. Lacking these aids to identification we are probably wise to accept the commonly held view that the species was not successfully introduced into cultivation until 1759. The important thing is to enjoy it – in the garden or at table.

Plate 59

Hemerocallis minor

Viola pedata L.

BIRD'S-FOOT VIOLET, CUT-LEAVED VIOLET, CROWFOOT VIOLET

FAMILY: Violaceae
DISTRIBUTION: eastern North America
CULTIVATION: hardy perennial but susceptible to late frosts; prefers well-drained, somewhat acid soil; propagated by division of the rhizome

THE genus *Viola* is so large and some of the species hybridize with such abandon that no botanist has yet been able to sort them out to everyone's satisfaction. The American botanist Ezra Brainerd devoted many years of research to the North American species, his work being continued by his daughter, suitably named Viola; and a German, Wilhelm Becker, spent thirty years studying the rest. Over a thousand species have been named and these divided into sixteen botanic sections and many sub-sections.

The pretty violet figured in the plate is in a sub-section all by itself because of its palmately divided leaves that resemble the marks of birds' feet in mud or snow. It also has an unusual style not evident in the plate but worth looking at through a hand glass in a living specimen. It is shaped like an Indian club with a dent at the top where there is a hole for the entry of pollen. The orange-topped anthers of the stamens are conspicuous but the plant does not often fertilize itself and relies upon insects that alight on the lower petal and make for the nectaries. It has a special device for ejecting its hard and slippery seeds. When the fruit is ripe the case hardens, forms up into a U-shape, and, as it dries and the available space gets smaller, the seeds are popped out of the top. The petals vary in colour but the leaves make it unmistakable.

With many other plants the Bird's-foot Violet was introduced from Virginia and was in cultivation by 1759. In England a great interest developed in colonial genera and not simply in economic plants. This plate was drawn in 1789 from a violet growing in a Hackney garden where there were many other American plants. The arch-romantic of the period, William Beckford, who built the extravagant folly Fonthill Abbey, had among his plantings an Alpine Garden and American Garden, and the latter is still to be found in parts of Great Britain today.

Plate 60

Viola pedata

Trillium sessile L.

SESSILE TRILLIUM

FAMILY: Liliaceae
DISTRIBUTION: central and eastern North America
CULTIVATION: hardy perennial; prefers a shady position and a humus-rich soil;
propagated by rhizome offsets or by seed

TRILLIUM species range widely through North America and they have less decorative species in Central and East Asia. Four species travelled east from the colonies in the 18th century, *T. sessile* with the lively common name of Toadshade was introduced to Europe in 1759 together with a taller and more odorous species, *T. erectum*, known as Birthroot. In Europe they all picked up the name American Herb Paris, not because they had anything to do with the French capital but because there was a parity in their flower parts. Linnaeus sensibly decided that *Trillium* was equally descriptive, the plants having three leaves, three sepals, and three petals. *T. sessile* has its name because it has no leaf or flower stalks. They simply emerge from the stem which gives it a crushed artificial appearance especially when they are seen from the side. But as the whole thing is only 15 centimetres (6 inches) high its wine-coloured flowers, sepals, and leaves are generally seen from above against a background of leafmould in the springtime. Then the blend of colours and the geometric arrangement of the plant parts truly strike the eye.

This was one of William Curtis's earlier, undated plates, but he proudly mentions that the actual plant we see figured was grown in his own botanic garden *'from roots sent me the preceding autumn by Mr. Robert Squibb, Gardener, of Charleston, South-Carolina'*. We know nothing whatever of Mr Squibb save that he was an indefatigable collector who sent to the Old World what riches he could find in the New.

The common liking of Trilliums and many of the first imported plants for moist woodland tells us how the American littoral might have looked before settlers began to reclaim land for husbandry. In time their original habitat was altered and so, with the Indians, they were driven further west. The leaves have been eaten as famine food and the dried rhizomes used by the Indians as herbal remedies. Indeed they were used for various purposes by American doctors until as recently as 1947, but are not acceptable today.

126

Plate 61

Trillium sessile

Lagerstroemia indica L.

INDIAN LILAC, CREPE MYRTLE

FAMILY: Lythraceae
DISTRIBUTION: eastern Asia from Korea to Indonesia and North Australia
CULTIVATION: non-hardy shrub or tree; better kept in a heated greenhouse in winter
and placed outdoors in summer; propagated by cuttings or by seed

A SMALL detail of one of the most attractive of all flowering Far Eastern shrubs is shown here.

A Dutch field botanist and a German working independently wrote the plant up at the beginning of the 18th century, both writing clear and easily identifiable descriptions but giving them local names, *Sibi* and *Tsjinkin*. A French Jesuit was the first to send a dried specimen in 1743 to the Royal Garden in Paris. It was left to Linnaeus to name the plant which he did in the tenth edition of his *Systema Naturae* published in 1759 honouring a close friend and compatriot and fellow naturalist, Magnus von Lagerstroem. He used the specific name *indica* as he frequently identified India with China. Lagerstroem well deserved the compliment for though he never travelled beyond Göteborg where he was Director of the Swedish East India Company he was of infinite service to Linnaeus as the enthusiastic importer of oriental scientific treasures ranging from herbarium material and living plants to a carved rhinoceros-horn drinking vessel said to detect poisons and increase potency. As he sent the plant named for him to Linnaeus, he may be regarded as its introducer into cultivation in the West.

Some species of *Lagerstroemia* grow to a great size and make good timber trees, but this hardy evergreen does not grow beyond 6 metres (20 feet), and generally is cut back and grown as a bush or standard. Being so easily cultivated by slips in sand it spread quickly from its native China and in the East is frequently found near temples. Commonly it is known as Crepe Myrtle or, on account of Linnaeus's peculiar mistake being perpetuated, as Indian Lilac, and it is found all over the world in warm climates. Possibly it is seen most often in Italy where it is used in street plantings, appears to tolerate fumes, neglect, and the depredations of hooligans with a surprising toughness, and requires the minimum of annual maintenance. Mostly the flowers are puce deepening to mauve, though there is a white variety.

Plate 62

Lagerstroemia indica

Aristolochia macrophylla Lam.

DUTCHMAN'S PIPE

FAMILY: Aristolochiaceae
SYNONYMS: *Aristolochia sipho* L'Hérit., *A. durior* Hill
DISTRIBUTION: eastern North America
CULTIVATION: hardy perennial climber; prefers loamy soil and some shade; propagated by seed or by cuttings

ARISTOLOCHIAS are weird-looking climbers. Their flowers are on long stalks and hang beneath a canopy of leaves undistinguished in colouring but tubular shaped. Some species are open at the top and resemble small euphoniums. Others, such as the species in the plate, are bent in a U-shape and nipped at the neck. For this reason they were called Dutchman's Pipe by the North American settlers. The upright flower contains no honey so pollinating insects are most probably attracted by its smell or colouring and penetrate into the tube. They find the inside is glassy and they cannot escape until they have done their pollinating. This done, the fertilized flower turns upside down and out slip the imprisoned insects.

Dutchman's Pipe was sent to Europe in 1763 by the first colonial-born botanist, John Bartram, who collected for patrons in Great Britain and founded the first botanic garden on the banks of the Schuylkill River. His father had reached the colonies '*before there was a single house in Philadelphia*', got himself disowned by the Quakers, and scalped by the Yamasee Indians. John was also ejected by the Quakers for not conforming and he bewildered them by blithely paying no attention. He was a good farmer, averaging 33 bushels of wheat an acre while his neighbours averaged only 20; but, then, one day he lost his heart to a colony of Bird's-foot Violets and determined to become a botanist. To the dismay of his wife he handed over the farm to a manager, learnt Latin and botany, found patrons in England, became the first American plant-hunter, and sent hundreds of native plants to Europe. There were serious losses in transit but his patrons still found their investment worth while. He dared greatly, often travelling alone, and after him his son William continued the work. Unlike most self-taught adventurers he won renown: George III appointed him King's Botanist of Philadelphia. Linnaeus declared him '*the greatest living botanist in the world*'. Bartram's botanic garden is still largely extant. He still lives to many gardeners in his numerous introductions to the Old World.

Plate 63

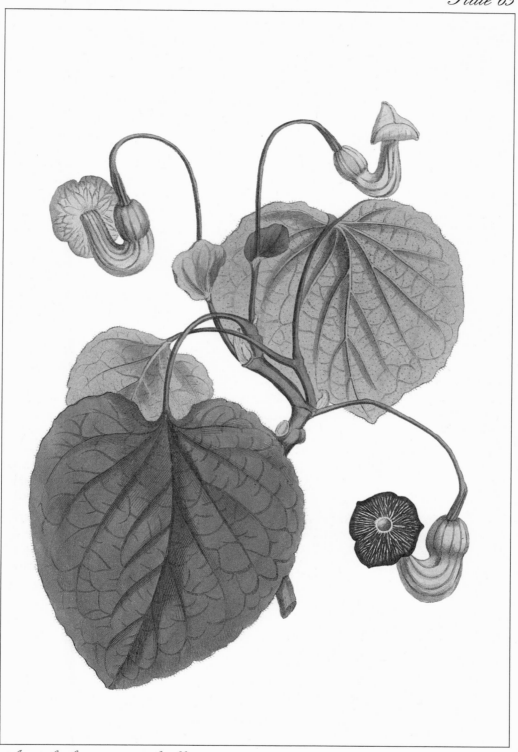

Aristolochia macrophylla

Rhododendron ponticum L.

PURPLE RHODODENDRON

FAMILY: Ericaceae
DISTRIBUTION: Asia Minor, Thrace, southern Spain and Portugal, naturalized
elsewhere
CULTIVATION: hardy evergreen shrub or tree; prefers well-drained but moist, acid,
humus-rich soil; propagated by cuttings or by seed

Two species of dwarf *Rhododendron*, both called Alpine Roses and pollinated by
humble-bees, are natives of the central European Alps, and were grown in gardens at
lower altitudes sometime before 1763 when the much taller *R. ponticum* turned up in
Spain and was introduced into cultivation. Its provenance was not limited to the
Iberian peninsular as it also grew in the Levant.

There is something about the genus that seizes plantsmen by the throat, and
Rhodendron men are as noticeably different from general gardeners as, say, Rosarians
or champion Parsnip-growers or those absorbed in the culture of Sweet Peas. A few
other Rhododendrons were introduced in the 18th century from North America and
the Caucasus but the Pontic species towered over them all in popularity and was the
primary cause of the new craze. By the end of the century it was one of the most
common of European shrubs, only unhappy where there was too much lime in the soil.
It grew like heather on the hills, rampageously. Its strength was utilized by
gamekeepers who planted it as undergrowth in coverts and as windbreaks or shelter
belts on the edge of woodland, and its virtual immunity to grime and fumes gave it
pride of place in the parks and gardens of the new industrial areas. Moreover, the
unmatchable vigour of the species made it the best of all stocks for grafting in scions of
weaker choice species. They are still used today, seed being sown in a sheltered site
and covered with Spruce boughs to give shade and protection until the young plants
appear. When they are the thickness of a pencil they are used as stocks for saddle-
grafting.

In isolation and looked after, a mature plant will make a trunk about 35 centimetres
(a foot) in diameter and have a spread of branches the size of a summer-house. But the
disadvantage of this otherwise excellent shrub has made itself apparent where plants
have been sited too closely, or not curbed, or temporarily abandoned. Then they
sucker and spread and, as they grow older, they form jungles that can only be cleared
by billhook, axe, and fire. Ironically, having subdued many a shrubbery and gone wild
beyond it this extensively planted species has crossed and re-crossed, and true stock of
the original Pontic Rhododendron is somewhat difficult to find.

Plate 64

Rhododendron ponticum

Kaempferia rotunda L.

FAMILY: Zingiberaceae
DISTRIBUTION: Indo-Malaysian region
CULTIVATION: non-hardy perennial; a stove plant that needs plenty of water when growing but as soon as the leaves turn yellow it must be kept dry for a few months; propagated by division of the rootstock

LINNAEUS honoured one early plant-collector by naming after him an exotic genus of the Ginger family. Engelbert Kaempfer was a Westphalian who sailed to the East as a surgeon in the fleet of the Dutch East India Company and from 1690 to 1692 he was stationed, or virtually imprisoned, in what must have been the most uncomfortable post belonging to the company: a tiny artificial island 75 metres by 215 (82 yards by 236), linked to Japan by a guarded causeway. The surgeon was allowed ashore only once a year on a formal visit to the ruling Shogun. Thwarted by his inability to botanize, he persuaded the Japanese officials to show him specimens by giving them free lessons in astronomy and mathematics, and he bribed the coolies with Dutch gin to bring him plants. His patience was rewarded by sufficient information to write and illustrate a work on Japanese plants that was published in 1714 and greatly excited Western botanists.

The showy species *K. rotunda* originally came from India and Java and since 1768 it has been grown in stoves or planted beneath trees in tropical gardens as ground cover. The plate is unusual in that the leaf is uncoloured. The text does not explain why. The flower spike is short and has between four and six blossoms though seldom more than two are in bloom at the same time. The lilac double lip constitutes a landing plane for insects. When the flowers die down the 20 centimetre (8 inch), oblong leaves, a muddy mixture of colours above and purple beneath, grow from short leaf stalks. The tubers are aromatic and have a hot gingery flavour.

The *Botanical Magazine* named this plant Round-rooted Galangale, no doubt because for centuries the pungent, aromatic root of plants from the genera *Alpinia* and *Kaempferia* were imported as a medicinal and culinary spice called galangale. Allegedly Arabs still use it to 'ginger up' their horses, presumably before horse fairs; and Russians use it for flavouring a liqueur. But to use the wide and loose term Galangale for *K. rotunda*, even though it does have aromatic tubers, is not all that sound; especially as a close species actually called *K. galanga* might reasonably be considered a source of the pungent spice, but it happens to have totally odourless tubers. To avoid such a muddle we judge it wiser to say there is no common name in English.

Plate 65

Kaempfera rotunda

Bergenia crassifolia (L.) Fritsch.

BERGENIA

FAMILY: Saxifragaceae
SYNONYM: *Saxifraga crassifolia* L.
DISTRIBUTION: Siberia and Korea
CULTIVATION: hardy perennial; flowers susceptible to late frosts; better planted in a
sheltered position; propagated by division of the rhizome

By coincidence two similar plates follow one another. Although the two plants they
figure were introduced to cultivation within a year of each other, almost fourteen years
and 724 plates lay between their publication. Yet both were engraved by Sansom –
and this is one out of the eight actually drawn by him – and both have uncoloured
leaves. The flower is well done, not in any sense a botanical drawing but accurate in
form so that the species can be identified by the infloresence with its spread flowers
mostly turned to one side hanging downwards. But it is a mystery that the leaf remains
uncoloured particularly as the plant is principally cultivated for its foliage. We see the
shape, like a canoe paddle, and we note the veining, but in perspective there is no depth
to show the size, density, or texture which led to it being given the specific *crassifolia*
from *crassus*, the Latin for solid, or thick, or heavy. The flowers give a show in spring
during March and April[1] but the leaves are of great ornamental value all the year
round. Being shining and leathery and a rich green they combine well with the right
type of cut flower and they last more than a month in water. In winter their green
darkens to a burnished rust colour and they turn green again in spring. In a garden they
make bold foils set against plants with different leaves. Compound leaves especially are
in strong contrast; but so are other simple leaves of different shape such as those like
swords, or halberds, or arrows, or crescents; and the polish of Bergenia leaves goes well
with leaves of a different texture, those that are pock-marked, or hairy, or powdered,
or felt-like. They make superb ground cover and are at their best in clumps or colonies
being altogether wasted as an edging plant.

The plant's original home was Siberia and, by way of Sweden, it found its way into
European gardens in 1765. It is noted that one of Linnaeus's disciples incurred his
displeasure by going on a botanical embassage to London and, liking the climate and the
opportunities for scientific research, failed to return. This was Dr Daniel Carl Solander
who played an increasingly important part in the history of English botany and
horticulture. It was he who introduced this Bergenia into the country of his adoption.

[1] Well-established hybrid descendants of this species, raised in 1950 by the German nursery of
George Arends, will sometimes flower a second time in autumn. They are *B.* 'Morgenröte' (Morning
Red), *B.* 'Abendglut' (Evening Glow), and *B.* 'Silberlicht' (Silver Light).

Plate 66

Bergenia crassifolia

Paeonia tenuifolia L.

FINE-LEAVED PAEONY

FAMILY: Paeoniaceae
DISTRIBUTION: south-east Europe and Asia Minor
CULTIVATION: hardy perennial; needs a warm, sunny position and sandy soil;
propagated by division of the rootstock

FORMERLY the Paeony belonged to the *Ranunculaceae* and was called '*loveliest of the buttercups*'. Now it is one genus with many species and cultivars in a family by itself. For centuries it was principally regarded as a medicinal plant, wrapped in superstition and attributed with outlandish properties: the power to shine like the moon at night, the power to protect shepherds and their flocks, to stave off tempests, and to take care of harvests. Dioscorides himself wrote that it 'is good against poisons and bewitchings and fears and devils and their assaults, and against a fever that comes with shivering'. It had to be harvested in a certain way and the traditions were passed down from Theophrastus to Pliny and Apuleius and ultimately reached John Gerard who wrote down: '*of necessitie it must be gathered in the night; for if any man shall pluck off the fruit in the daytime, being sene of the Woodpecker, he is in danger to lose his eies.*' Gerard frankly considered this to be nonsense but then, apparently unaware that it contains a potentially dangerous drug, he went on to prescribe Paeony seeds in wine for those in a depressed state. For centuries the seeds and pieces of dried root were strung on necklaces and used as amulets against evil spirits, and as dummies for children to chew on and help them through teething, while the author of a cookery book of 1796 blithely wrote: '*Stick the cream with Paeony kernels.*' We must infer that any fatal mistakes went undiagnosed.

Of the many species and cultivars it was *P. tenuifolia*, a native of East Europe and the Caucasus, that was first grown commercially by a London nurseryman in 1765. It is smaller than most Paeonies, growing only to about 65 centimetres (2 feet), and has a cup-shaped flower of deep crimson. Above this it has the bounty of finely cut foliage. As much as anything this resembles the leaves of Giant Fennel. The combination of flowers and lace-patterned leaves give it the highest crown in a very regal race of plants.

Plate 67

Paeonia tenuifolia

Chimonanthus praecox (L.) Link

JAPAN ALLSPICE

FAMILY: Calycanthaceae
SYNONYM: *Calycanthus praecox* L.
DISTRIBUTION: China
CULTIVATION: hardy shrub; as the flowers may be damaged by severe frosts it is therefore better planted in a sheltered position; propagated by cuttings

HERE is an English common name that needs to be used with care for the plant's provenance is China not Japan, and Allspice might be confused with *Calycanthus floridus*, the Californian Allspice, or the Allspice Tree, *Pimenta officinalis*, the fruits of which are used in pickles, desserts, and the manufacture of Benedictine and Chartreuse liqueurs. It is a fragrant early-flowering species of a tiny genus of oriental plants much sought after by winter gardeners. The flowers, though unisexual, cannot pollinate themselves because the female stigma is receptive, so to speak, before the male anthers have grown up and matured sufficiently to produce pollen. Therefore the job has to be done by an outsider and a species of beetle carries ripe pollen from one plant to another. The flowers are a muddle of petals and sepals almost impossible to differentiate. The yellow parts are sepals and outer petals, the smaller bruise-coloured parts are inner petals. Not only are the flowers scented but the bark is also aromatic and it is much used in the orient for decking hair and for scenting linen. It was first discovered growing in China by a Portuguese Jesuit, Alvarus de Semedo, who wrote it up under the name of *La mei* together with a variety of other plants in 1633. Almost eighty years later Kaempfer saw a specimen in Japan, noted it had been introduced there from China and that the scent could be somewhat overpowering. Simultaneously a Scot, James Cunningham, collected and dried a specimen in China, calling it *La boe*, which found its way home and can still be examined in the British Museum. The first, however, to grow a living specimen in Europe in 1766 was the then Earl of Coventry, a botanical enthusiast whose country house had a large conservatory. Within a dozen years his seedling had begun to bloom. Within thirty-three it had grown 5.5 metres (16 feet) high and 3.5 metres (10 feet) wide, was covered in blossoms in the winter, and gave off such a fragrance it could be smelt fifty metres from the conservatory. He grew other specimens outside, and it is largely from his stock that English nurserymen obtained layered cuttings and seeds for introducing the plant into European gardens.

The plate is prettily designed but invites a query as to why a full-grown leaf is shown attached to a flowering and budding twig, for it is a feature of this species that it flowers through the winter before putting out its leaves.

Plate 68

Chimonanthus praecox

Moraea tristis (L. fil.) Ker.-Gawl.

MORAEA

FAMILY: Iridaceae
SYNONYM: *Iris tristis* L. fil.
DISTRIBUTION: South Africa
CULTIVATION: perennial corm; generally hardy but it is better to lift the corms in winter; propagated by corm offsets or by seed

MORAEAS come from the Southern hemisphere; a single species from Australia, a few from the Mascarenes to the east of Madagascar, and the remaining ninety or so from tropical and temperate South Africa. Their blossoming is fleeting but new ones quickly follow and a clump will flower for some weeks. In appearance they are not unlike their close relatives the Iris. The most brilliant are rightly named Peacock Moraeas, with three large petals and three little ones each with an eye of iridescent blue, and of many shades: dark and light blue, orange, red, yellow, lilac, lemon, and white. Other species are smaller and less conspicuous, of which *M. tristis* is a good contrasting example. Its stem seldom reaches 30 centimetres (a foot) and it has between four to six flowers the colour of rappee snuff with a deep yellow eye. Its thin leaves grow to about 60 centimetres (2 feet). A part not shown is its corm skirted with a net of fibres. Gardeners who enjoy bright colours might consider it a very poor relation of the gaudy Peacock Moraeas. The *Botanical Magazine* suggested an unlovely English name, Dull-coloured Flag. In translation the Latin specific name is as bad, the Mournful or Dejected Moraea. But the plant has admirers because its colours are quiet and its appearance interesting. A few will go so far as to regard it as elegant and a collector's piece.

The species was being grown in England in 1768 from an anonymous introduction from the Cape of Good Hope. A second and more thorough introduction to Europe was affected by one of Linnaeus's close friends, Karl Peter Thunberg, who botanized at the Cape from 1772 for almost three years and sent back herbarium collections and living plants to Uppsala. He was on his way to Java, thence travelling to the close confines of the island off Japan where Kaempfer had done his stint, cleverly collecting specimens from the animal fodder and litter brought in daily from the mainland. He returned by way of Ceylon, then Dutch territory, Holland, England, and Germany; and when both Linnaeus and his son had died, he took their place as Professor of Botany at Uppsala. Of all the botanic apostles sent out by Linnaeus to scour the world for plants Thunberg was perhaps the most adventurous and successful.

Plate 69

Moraea tristis

Dionaea muscipula Ellis

VENUS'S FLY-TRAP

FAMILY: Droseraceae
DISTRIBUTION: North America: confined to the coastal region of Carolina
CULTIVATION: half-hardy perennial; requires moist, acid soil and high air humidity, in winter it must be kept cold but not frozen; propagated by seed, division of the rootstock is not recommended

PLANTS that react rapidly to outside stimuluses can be startling. At the slightest touch the Squirting Cucumber snaps from its stalk, explodes, and scatters its seeds over a large area. Many of the Balsams, especially the Himalayan species, have fruit capsules with elastic valves that, at a touch, fire off their black seeds with great force. The leaflets of the Sensitive and Humble Plants collapse and fold. The stamens of a Barberry, touched by an insect, promptly fall inwards and the anthers powder the intruder with pollen. All these are reproductive or defensive mechanisms. The Venus's Fly-trap is precisely what it says it is: a carnivorous plant that catches and holds insects. Like the *Sarracenia* figured as Plate 54 it is a North American plant and its habitat is swampy ground. Therefore it has the same need for nitrogen that it cannot obtain in a conventional manner and digests it from the animal tissue of insects. The leaves are arranged in a rosette and are between 2.5 and 12.5 centimetres (1 and 5 inches) long. They are divided into two parts, the outward section resembling open iron-maidens or set man traps, or gins. They are oblong or quadrangular with serrated green edges and each side of the trap has three hairs all marvellously designed with a joint so that they can collapse and lie flat when the trap is sprung by a passing or curious insect. Within a fraction of a second the leaves close until the two sides are tightly pressed together, and red glands that can only be seen through a hand glass begin to secrete a fermenting fluid and pump it over the prey. After the plant has absorbed all it needs the leaf opens again. Above this wonderful demonstration of rapid reaction an umbel of flowers blooms in high summer. They are pretty, but not sufficiently to earn the plant a place in a collection, yet, as an example of Divine ingenuity, it has been carefully grown in botanic gardens and by private enthusiasts since its introduction to Europe from Carolina in 1768.

Plate 70

Dionaea muscipula

Camellia sinensis (L.) O. Kuntze

TEA

FAMILY: Theaceae
SYNONYMS: *Thea sinensis* L., *Camellia thea* Link, *C. bohea* L., *C. theifera* (Griff.) Dyer
DISTRIBUTION: eastern Himalayas and Hainan, cultivated elsewhere
CULTIVATION: half-hardy tree or shrub; it requires lime-free, aluminium-rich soil, high air humidity and some shade, it tolerates some frost and should not be kept too warm in winter, nor too hot in summer; propagated by cuttings and by seed

THE tea we drink is a plant of Chinese or Indian origin that will grow into a small tree in the wild. In commerce it is kept pruned to a small bush and various pickings are made as often as is feasible. In Ceylon it is done every ten to twelve days throughout the year. The bud and top two leaves make pekoe teas; the coarser leaves are used for souchongs and congous. They are dried in withering houses, pressed a little in rollers, and, except for the green teas and gunpowder, are then fermented, rolled again, fired, and sifted into grades. Blenders then step in. At length the dried leaves reach the consumer; the biggest tea-drinkers being the Slavs, the British, and the Orientals; and its brewing or infusion of is invested with esoteric rites. *C.s.* var. *assamica* has larger leaves but is otherwise the same as the plant in the plate.

Tea has been drunk in the Far East for thousands of years and legends abound as to how it began. Most infer that this exhilarating and pleasant infusion was discovered entirely by accident which is surely true of most food and drink. The plant was written up by some early experts: first in 1623 in Switzerland by Caspar Bauhin who named it Chaa.[1] It is alleged that the Dutch introduced the beverage to continental Europe and even to America before it reached England in 1752. For a long time it was a rich man's drink. In England 'tay' was 'taken' in porcelain dishes without handles and was very fashionable. In 1757 the first Tea House was established in London, a social-political 'club' not to be confused with its modern Japanese namesake. In Russia and the Balkans the dried tea leaves were brewed in samovars and drunk from tumblers. Living specimens were introduced by 1768 and grown in greenhouses because out of doors they never managed to flower. Their fragrant and chalky flowers had an appeal but they could not compete with *C. japonica* that, after one early abortive attempt, was successfully introduced from Japan in 1792. This Camellia was of such magnificence that the Tea Plant's nose was swiftly put out of joint.

---

[1] 'Cha' remains the London Cockney dialect for tea.

Plate 71

Camellia sinensis

Hippeastrum vittatum (L'Hérit.) Herb.

HIPPEASTRUM

FAMILY: Amaryllidaceae
SYNONYM: *Amaryllis vittata* L'Hérit.
DISTRIBUTION: South America: mountains of Peru and western Brazil
CULTIVATION: non-hardy bulbous plant; needs warmth, may be cultivated in a greenhouse or on a windowsill, after flowering it should not be watered; propagated by bulb offsets or by seed

LINNAEUS'S son who succeeded dynastically to his chair of Botany asserted this greenhouse plant was an Amaryllis; a mistake perpetuated by the majority of present-day bulb sellers in their catalogues. Indeed it is but one of many plants loosely termed 'Amaryllis' although there is only one, the Belladonna Lily. It was introduced to Europe in 1769 by a London nurseryman, and very likely a mistake was made in labelling or in recording the provenance of bulbs, for William Curtis himself considered it probably came from the Cape. In fact it must have been in a consignment from America because its provenance is the high Peruvian Andes, and all seventy-five species of the genus come from tropical and subtropical South America. *H. vittatum* is a common flower on the Mediterranean littoral where it needs no attention at all, is virtually evergreen, and grows to a metre (3 feet) with a spread of between three and six massive flower trumpets. It is also a superb cut flower, lasting three weeks in a large vase. The plate is good but does not quite convey the majesty of the plant. It has six or eight leaves that are leek-coloured, up to 10 centimetres (4 inches) wide and bluntly pointed. They grow like the fan-shaped leaves of a Talipot Palm, one on top of the other, and they are prominent from the time the flowers begin to die down in late June until the following March. Only for a very short time is there no evidence of the plant above ground. In less bland climates it needs protection and is never quite so effective.

Less than twenty years after its arrival in Europe an English watchmaker had crossed it with another species, *H. reginae*. By skilful, and no doubt secret, processes he stabilized his hybrid until its progeny produced uniform characteristics: four blooms on a 60 centimetre (2 foot) stem with flowers chiefly scarlet, streaked with white and with green at the throat of the trumpet. It bears the watchmaker's name *H.* × *johnsonii*, and as a pot plant it is one of the easiest Hippeastrums to cultivate. Both *H. vittatum* and its descendant *H.* × *johnsonni* are infinitely more graceful than the modern, chunky hybrids on tall stems the thickness of a forefinger bred chiefly in Holland and for which the trade grubs about for fresh and somewhat incredible superlatives.

Plate 72

Hippeastrum vittatum

Sophora tetraptera T. Miller

WINGED-PODDED SOPHORA, KOWHAI

FAMILY: Leguminosae
SYNONYM: *Edwardsia grandiflora* Salisb.
DISTRIBUTION: New Zealand (North Island, from East Cape to lat. 40° 30′ S.), Lord
Howe Isles, and Chile
CULTIVATION: half-hardy tree, normally evergreen but looses its leaves after frost; it
needs some protection in winter; propagated by seed; it hybridizes with *Sophora
microphylla*

IN 1757 a small boy at Eton named Joseph Banks took a solitary walk after bathing
and was suddenly struck by the beauty of the hedge flowers. It was more than a mere
romantic experience for he was to have a great impact upon the world of natural
science. Becoming very rich, very influential and being a great organizer, he was to
dominate the Royal Society for years, make Kew known all over the world, and send
out professional collectors to amass rich collections and introduce many plants from all
the continents. But he was not simply a Maecenas who sent out plant-hunters. He
went on three expeditions himself, the most notable and productive in 1768 when,
together with Linnaeus's 'lost' friend, Dr Solander, two assistants, four servants, and a
pair of greyhounds, he sailed from Plymouth in a converted Yorkshire collier,
Endeavour, on Captain Cook's first voyage round the world. Banks had contributed
£10,000 to the expedition and so was given special quarters, but comforts were
minimal. There was little privacy and always danger from disease. Moreover, they
sailed some of the worst seas on the globe and were exposed to extremes of heat and
cold, calm and gales. They were shipwrecked and saved by a chance in a million. In
that long voyage a third of the ship's complement died, but the rewards were very
great. Cook filled in many places on the map, and the collections of Banks and Solander
amazed scientific Europe. They had innumerable insects, fish, skins of birds, dried and
preserved plants, drawings, and viable seeds. Amongst the last were those of the
Sophora or Kowhai Tree found in New Zealand in 1769. Solander prophesied
correctly it would be one of the most popular of their introductions and noted the
peculiar way it was pollinated – by the frantic action of Parson-birds that hurled
themselves at the trees to sip at the quantities of nectar, greedily tearing at the flowers
and pollinating the survivors. In its native habitat it grows to 13 metres (40 feet),
though elsewhere it scarcely reaches 10 metres (30 feet). Nevertheless it is a useful
and decorative tree to plant in a protected position. The ferny foliage is particularly
esteemed; so are the golden flowers, their shape like a marriage of Sweet Peas and
Fuchsias. The seeds are contained in a vessel with four wings which resembles a
necklace. The wood is valuable to cabinet-makers and joiners and so hard that it can be
used for shafts.

Plate 73

Sophora tetraptera

Acacia myrtifolia (Smith) Willd.

MYRTLE-LEAVED MIMOSA

FAMILY: Leguminosae
SYNONYM: *Mimosa myrtifolia* Smith
DISTRIBUTION: Australia and Tasmania
CULTIVATION: half-hardy shrub; requires a well-drained, sunny position and
protection in winter; propagated by seed or by cuttings

THE Banks and Solander collections from Captain Cook's circumnavigation were of primary interest because they came from many places as yet untouched by botanical explorers. True, a most unusual plant-hunter, William Dampier,[1] had landed in New Holland (as Australia was then called) and he returned to Europe in 1699 with plant drawings and dried specimens, and to him is attributed the introduction of the Parrotbeak Glory Pea. But it is nevertheless a fact that Linnaeus's *Species Plantarum* included no species from Australia. The voyage of the *Endeavour* inaugurated a new era in the introduction of exotics, and few plants could be considered more Australian than *Acacia*. The genus has a huge number of species that have many uses, among them gums, tanbarks, dyes, scents, detergents, shampoos, fibres, ink, and timber for all sorts of purposes from the construction of wheels and yokes to spears and boomerangs. In southern Australia especially *Acacia* species can manage with so little water that they form a large percentage of the bush scrub. In cultivation they make impenetrable hedges, windbreaks, and provide nectar for bees. The first settlers made temporary wattle and daub buildings using *Acacia* slapped over with mud or a mixture of mud and lime with horse combings mixed in to bind the two, and roofed the place with bark shingles. Regrettably they later added quantities of clapboard and replaced the bark with galvanized iron thereby creating the unmistakable Australian sheep station style of architecture. Regrettably, too, in Australia the ugly name of Wattle fell on all species of *Acacia*. Generally in Europe it is called Mimosa.

Most Mimosa have easily recognisable bipinnate leaves but about a third of the species do not. *A. myrtifolia* shown here is an example. Though its specific name suggests it has leaves like those of a Myrtle it has none at all. Those oval 'leaves' prettily piped with a red edging are actually expanded and flattened leaf stalks and their edges turn upwards to expose less surface to radiation. The fragrant, ball-shaped lemon flowers are characteristic of the genus. How soon the species reached European stoves and gardens after the voyage of the *Endeavour* is not certain, but clearly it was early in the New Holland era of plant introduction.

---

[1] Dampier lived from 1652 to 1715 and, besides managing to get himself court-martialled for cruelty in the Royal Navy, his experiences also included being a logger in Yucatan, a fêted author, a noted hydrographer, navigator, and botanist, and a pirate chief.

Plate 74

Acacia myrtifolia

Lonicera implexa Ait.

HONEYSUCKLE

FAMILY: Caprifoliaceae
DISTRIBUTION: Mediterranean region
CULTIVATION: somewhat tender, evergreen, woody climber; can be planted out of doors but needs protection from severe frosts; propagated by cuttings or by seed

MONSIEUR Richard, Royal Gardener to the aged Louis XV, and in charge of the formal allées and bosquets and geometric gardens and stoves at Versailles, was responsible for the introduction of *Lonicera implexa* from woods and hedges about the Mediterranean into European gardens. Because of its provenance it needed a modicum of protection but less than the American Trumpet Honeysuckle and it was an attractive alternative to the climbing species then in cultivation, being firmly evergreen while others were not, and less vigorous and therefore less likely to get out of hand. Moreover, it had a distinct shade of red suffused in the cream-yellow of its flowers and bore the most handsome fruit. Unlike some species these berries are never joined to one another but quite separate. The foliage is interesting in that the opposite leaves are connate[1] and joined to form a cup round the stem as inseparable as Siamese twins, so much so that they can hold drops of dew or rain. The flowers are equally interesting because the group of closed flowers, shown in the lowest cluster, go through elaborate gyrations to ensure fertilization. The flower is between 2.5 and 5 centimetres (1 and 2 inches) long and therefore the pollinating insect must have a very long proboscis to get at the nectary in the base. Before the flower actually opens the anthers on top of the stamens begin to unfold so that the two come into position to make the shape of a nail-head. They emerge as the flower opens and all move into a horizontal position. This is convenient for the insect who alights on the wobbling anthers and, while he is working his proboscis down to the honey, he becomes fluffy with pollen. Simultaneously, the style, which has been bent downwards, unwinds to its full height above the anthers. This means the flower might conceivably be self-pollinated, but it is unlikely. The insect will either go to another plant for a sip of honey and carry out the work of pollination there, or, just as likely, he will pollinate the next flowers to open on the same plant because buds break readily at regular intervals. The Mediterranean Honeysuckle must be one of the best-looking, most fragrant, and sweetest pieces of botanical machinery in existence.

[1] The Swiss scholar Johann Kaspar Orelli discovered a Latin inscription that most precisely describes the intimacy of being connate: *ET* (QUI) *CONNATVS FVERINT DE CONIUGE MEA.*

Plate 75

Lonicera implexa

Aethephyllum pinnatifidum (L. fil.) N.E.Br.

JAGGED-LEAVED FIG-MARIGOLD

FAMILY: Aizoaceae
SYNONYMS: *Mesembryanthemum pinnatifidum* L. fil., *Cleretum pinnatifidum* (L.fil.)
Bolus, *Micropterum pinnatifidum* (L.fil.)Schwant.
DISTRIBUTION: South Africa: Cape Province
CULTIVATION: an annual for a cool greenhouse or for planting out of doors in summer;
it requires a sunny position and loose, sandy soil

IN strong contrast to the splendid Strelitzia figured on Plate 80, *Aethephyllum pinnatifidum* has the charm of simplicity. Indeed, through half-closed eyes it bears a vague resemblance to a humble Hawkbit or a Groundsel. Karl Peter Thunberg was officially employed as surgeon by the Dutch East India Company and partly financed by Dutch horticulturalists, but he was Linnaeus's disciple first and last and during his stay at the Cape between 1772 and 1775 he made several journeys into the interior, collected about 300 new species, and sent seeds and herbarium material home to Sweden. In return he received long and eager letters from his master who bade him not to be afraid of taking a risk or two for the botanical laurels that one day were bound to crown his brow, and the direction: *'Lay for me a wreath of flowers on the altar of African Flora.'* Among Thunberg's introductions from the Cape was this small and unpretentious plant that was successfully established in the Uppsala Botanic Garden. Linnaeus decided that the plant was a Mesembryanthemum doubtless because some species of that huge genus had the same glistening hoar-frost appearance that reflect the sun's rays. Finally, South African botanists have put Thunberg's find into a genus of its own and there is only the one species.

Like many plants that exist in arid habitats, the *Aethephyllum* makes full use of dew and seasonal torrents of rain and relies upon moisture for the dissemination of its seeds. A fruit is shown in the lower part of the plate. This is a capsule with five separate chambers. They open under the pressure of valves that operate only when they are wet. Moreover, they are capable of repeatedly opening and shutting so that the seeds within have the best possible chance of ripening and becoming properly viable before they are scattered and, as they are popped out on to ground already moistened, they stand the best chance of germinating.

Plate 76

Aethephyllum pinnatifidum

Monsonia Lobata Mont.

BROAD-LEAVED MONSONIA

FAMILY: Geraniaceae
DISTRIBUTION: South Africa
CULTIVATION: non-hardy sub-shrub; requires a heated greenhouse; propagated by
cuttings or by seed

DURING 1774 seeds and plants flooded from the Cape into Europe and the subject
of this plate and the following five were all introduced in that one year through the
agency of the botanist Thunberg or the Kew under-gardener Masson. They did not
have the field to themselves. Simultaneously two Scotch amateurs were collecting, and
a Dutchman named Ange, shrewdly judging the market, both guided plant-hunters for
a fee and made collections himself, selling living plants and birds, herbarium material,
and other sets of exsiccata to passing travellers or to rich patrons in Europe. There was
also a young Swede named Oldenburg, described variously as a surgeon's mate and as a
private soldier, who botanized and helped both Thunberg and Masson until that same
year of 1774 he died in delirious convulsions of a fever in Madagascar.

There are many Monsonias with a wide distribution, but the two most commonly
found in gardens, *M. lobata* and *M. speciosum*, are both Cape plants and were both sent
home by Masson. *M. lobata* figured here is the larger, and the other species has cut-up
leaves. In their native land Monsonias have three names: Slangbom, Snake-flower, and
Lady Monson. The last is not quite accurate as Linnaeus named the genus for one of
his correspondents, a Lady Anne Monson, described as 'a very superior whist-player'
and an enthusiastic botanist, who in that rich year of 1774, was actually collecting at
the Cape. But the old master at Uppsala, now 67, was not merely complimenting a
fellow naturalist. It was the year of his silver wedding to his unsuitable wife and
'botanic loves' were no longer enough. He declared himself in a letter to Lady Anne
whom he had never met: '*I have long been trying to smother a passion which has proved
unquenchable and which now has burst into flame* . . . ' He called her a phoenix amongst
women, sent her *Alstromeria* seeds, and made the quaint proposal: '*that I may be
permitted to join with you in the procreation of just one little daughter to bear witness of our love
– a little Monsonia, through which your fame would live for ever* . . . '

This is their child. Poor old gentleman.

Plate 77

Monsonia lobata

Aridaria viridiflora (Ait.) Bolus

GREEN FIG-MARIGOLD

FAMILY: Aizoaceae
SYNONYM: *Mesembryanthemum viridiflorum* Ait.
DISTRIBUTION: South Africa
CULTIVATION: non-hardy perennial; requires scarcely any water when resting, then must be watered from below; it does best in a sunny position in a cool greenhouse, well rooted in loose, sandy loam with excellent drainage; propagated by seed or by cuttings

BY 1774 when Masson sent this green-flowered plant from the Cape to the Royal Gardener at Kew, it was put into the *Mesembryanthemum* genus, seventy of which were already in cultivation and which varied enormously. All were leaf succulents but some had flat, broad, tapered leaves; others were shaped like small cylinders; others were formed in a clump and looked like miniature Hostas; yet others were a flat star of leaves resting on the desert; and some, called 'window-plants', had a single pair of leaves shaped convexly. These and complex botanical differences have resulted in a recent splitting of the genus into many genera, and the Green Fig-marigold has been placed among the *Aridaria*. But *Mesembryanthemum* is still the portmanteau word used by generations of gardeners. Almost without exception they have cheerful colours which makes the green-flowered species a specialist's flower. More than anything else the thinly petalled flowers resemble Snake-locks Sea Anemones and they slightly differ in shade from the pairs of leaves and the stems that are shining and dotted with reflecting blobs.

A. viridiflora was keenly appreciated by an English authority on succulents who gave his name to one genus, *Haworthia*. In his work on Mesembryanthemums, published in 1784, Mr Haworth named it *M. viridiflorum*, lavished praise on the green petals, and employed a striking fungus simile to describe them in corruption: '*they decay, coalesce and melt into a pulpy mass, and become almost as soft a matter as the aged gills of a deliquescent agaric.*' The seeds, he noted, were kidney-shaped but not numerous, and he had never found ripe ones. *A. Viridiflora* did well by Mr Haworth who was an assiduous collector,[1] a good observer, and thorough. He also had sufficient self-confidence to apostrophize his readers. Not unlike Micawber in *David Copperfield* he pugnaciously challenged people to appreciate him. '*If but the germinating rudiments of merit are discovered in the foregoing OBSERVATIONS . . . I shall be encouraged to extend them to other orders of succulent plants. If NOT, let silence content me!! — Let my Botanical readers examine and judge!! — Let the Public decide!!! — '* Evidently Adrian Hardy Haworth was something of a Caesar among naturalists.

---

[1] He married thrice, had many children, and died the possessor of 20,000 herbarium specimens and 40,000 insects.

Plate 78

Aridaria viridiflora

Protea repens (L.) L.

SUGARBUSH

FAMILY: Proteaceae
SYNONYM: *Protea mellifera* Thunb.
DISTRIBUTION: South Africa
CULTIVATION: non-hardy evergreen shrub or tree; needs plenty of light, abundant ventilation, and a loose, lime-free soil allowing perfect drainage; it does not like being disturbed and is propagated by seed or by cuttings

PROTEUS, an ancient sea god who herded seals, had the power to take on different forms to elude those who wished to consult him; becoming a tiger or a lion, or disappearing in lightning, in a whirlwind, or in a rushing stream. His versatility was recalled by Linnaeus who named for him the gorgeous plants sent by Thunberg to Sweden and Holland and by Masson to England because they were in such an assortment of shapes and sizes. They also had a puzzling structure. What appeared to be petals were really coloured bracts arranged in a head not unlike a Teasel or an Artichoke. The true flowers are densely packed inside the bracts and look like hairs. In dissection the sepals and petals make a long tubular perianth and the stamens have plenty of pollen. Nevertheless they are not fertilized by wind but by insects or birds, probably because they are native to a dry climate where wind pollination would be wasteful and probably fail. The leaves have an extra skin and a down of hairs helping to check transpiration.

In the species here figured the leaves are short and thin and not hairy, but a waxy covering and their smallness protects them from great heat. The plant grows to a height of 2.7 metres (8 feet) in a well-ventilated, cool greenhouse. The Cape name, Sugarbush, emphasizes that it literally drips with nectar. It was used by the first European settlers in South Africa as a sweetening agent.

On their introduction Proteas became a fashionable plant, but only for rich gardeners or endowed botanic gardens because they were treated almost exclusively as stove plants. They thrived, and great collections were built up until the stoves were 'improved' by new heating systems and watering exotics became the practice. Even the most experienced gardeners advised that Proteas should never be short of water. The result was slow debilitation then decimation. Proteas virtually disappeared. No one even troubled to grow them in South African gardens until fairly recently. Then the real needs of the genus became known through intelligent experiments and they are grown again, not, however, in such quantity as at the end of the 18th century and the beginning of the 19th. They make popular cut flowers, but these are chiefly flown to world markets from South Africa.

Plate 79

Protea repens

Strelitzia reginae Banks

BIRD OF PARADISE FLOWER, BIRD'S TONGUE FLOWER

FAMILY: Strelitziaceae (Musaceae)
DISTRIBUTION: South Africa: Cape Province
CULTIVATION: non-hardy perennial, suitable for a heated greenhouse; requires a rich, rather heavy soil; propagated by suckers or by seed (to obtain seed the flowers must be artificially pollinated)

ONLY a few months after Captain Cook's first circumnavigation he was ordered to make a second. Joseph Banks decided to go too. He planned to take a suite of fifteen and at his expense a round-house was built aboard Cook's ship. This was so cumbersome that it put the vessel out of trim and on her trials she threatened to turn turtle. Banks was thwarted and angry. Deprived of his round-house he changed his mind, let Cook find another naturalist, and went off to Iceland instead. On his return he began the organisation of the English scientific world. Solander was his chief lieutenant. Dr Jonas Dryander, another Swede, was his librarian and custodian of his Cabinet of Natural History. Without delay Banks arranged for Kew to despatch an under-gardener, Francis Masson, to collect where he and Solander had personally observed an abundantly rich flora, the Cape of Good Hope. Masson arrived at the Cape in 1772, not long after Karl Thunberg, and the *Botanical Magazine* figured many of his successful plant introductions. The first and most remarkable was the Bird of Paradise Flower, named *Strelitzia reginae* by Banks in honour of George III's Queen, Charlotte of Mecklenburg-Strelitz. All five species of the genus are South African but *S. reginae*, the best known, has travelled far and is used extensively as a cut flower. A single bloom with one leaf in a vase is quite sufficient for some connoisseurs who feel that a mass of them is overwhelming. It seems appropriate that Los Angeles, one of the most overwhelming places on earth, should have adopted it as the city flower, and cohorts of Strelitzias are planted in the streets. The structure takes a little sorting out. The flowers emerge one at a time from a 20-centimetre (8-inch) sheath of green with an edge of red. Each flower has three orange sepals and three ink-coloured petals. One of the latter is small, the other two tall and joined together to make an arrowhead that contains anthers and nectar. When a bird lands on the arrow to get at the honey, the petals open and pollen is released, not in a fine cloud but matted together, and is swept away to fertilize another flower.

For the chronological order of this plate see Introduction, page 3.

Gardenia rothmannia L.

SPOTTED GARDENIA

FAMILY: Rubiaceae
DISTRIBUTION: South Africa
CULTIVATION: non-hardy evergreen shrub or tree; it needs a well-drained, dry, warm, and lime-free soil; propagated by cuttings

THUNBERG and Masson both introduced this species into cultivation in 1774. The genus is named for a botanist from Carolina, named Alexander Garden, and belongs to the Madder family of plants. In the 19th and 20th centuries Gardenias have been an acceptable alternative to the white Carnation, Camellia, or Orchid worn as a buttonhole with formal evening dress, but these were the highly scented, tightly petalled *G. jasminoides*, a species native to the Orient but which has been grown on such a scale in the sympathetic South African climate that it almost appears to belong there. The eleven South African species of Gardenia are double- or triple-coloured, and more open-petalled. The plate figuring *G. rothmannia*, arguably the most supreme, is unusually designed by Sydenham Edwards in that he deliberately cut off the leaves on the left. Its flower tube, with the coloured freckles and spectacular anthers and pistil, measures up to 5 centimetres (2 inches) in diameter and is so fragrant that the scent is detectable long after a specimen has been pressed and dried for an herbarium. The Gardenia is fairly uncommon among flowering shrubs in that it has single blossoms at the end of its branches that do not hang like a bell but look up to the sun. The evergreen leaves are hairy beneath and are arranged in groups of three, one not equal in size to the others. In South Africa the shrubs grow to a good height and make an iron-hard, white wood excellent for axe-hafts or knife-handles, and they were used primitively for spears. But the older the shrub grows the less flowers it produces and a professional grower or gardener is advised to make replacements every two to three years, striking cuttings at regular intervals to ensure continuity. The bushes enjoy heat and moisture and would be the easiest of shrubs to grow in a greenhouse if insects and funguses were not so fond of precisely the same conditions.

Strelitzia reginae

Plate 80

Plate 81

Gardenia rothmannia

Oxalis versicolor L.

STRIPED-FLOWER'D WOOD-SORREL

FAMILY: Oxalidaceae
DISTRIBUTION: South Africa: Cape Province
CULTIVATION: non-hardy herb; better kept as a pot plant in a cool greenhouse, it needs a sunny position; propagated by bulb offsets

THE tart taste of Sorrel sap is very like that of an *Oxalis* species, which accounts partly for the generic name, from the Greek for acid, and for its common name, Wood-Sorrel. There are more than 800 species now found almost all over the world, spread by various means from their original homes. The hand of man has played a large part in this distribution for scientific, aesthetic, and commercial reasons. As an example of the last, species *O. deppei* with a roundish bulb that is eaten in its native Mexico has become a favourite house-plant in Continental Europe because it has four leaflets like a lucky Shamrock and is a common New Year's gift. Man may have played the larger part in spreading the genus, but its own determination to breed and multiply should also be borne in mind. It is one of the most fecund of plants. Not content with root propagation – and there are species with creeping root-stocks, bulb-like stem bases, root- and axil-bulbils, real bulbs, and round rhizomes – they also have a most effective mechanism for seed dispersal. The fruit is a capsule with openings for its many seeds. Each seed sits in a covering structure that is like a glove finger half turned inside out. When it is ripe moisture from below builds up pressure until the glove finger abruptly turns the right way out and hurls the seed with considerable force a large distance. This ensures that the plant quickly spreads and *Oxalis* species make weed-blankets and pretty ground cover, but, in their steady surge over the globe, some species have become pests. The species figured here, which was in Masson's 1774 introduction, has never fallen in that category as it is fairly tender and very early was designated as a greenhouse plant. By careful management, however, potted plants could be in flower for most of the year and, as the plate shows, the flowers have the advantage of being quite as delightful closed as when they are open. At first they are red and yellow spirals like sticks of rock. As they uncurl the edges are seen to be red. Finally the five rounded petals open and lie flat to resemble silky white buttons edged with violet.

Plate 82

Oxalis versicolor

Pelargonium glaucum L'Hérit.

SPEAR-LEAVED GERANIUM, PELARGONIUM

FAMILY: Geraniaceae
SYNONYM: *Geranium lanceolatum* Cav.
DISTRIBUTION: South Africa
CULTIVATION: non-hardy sub-shrub; a suitable plant for the cool greenhouse;
propagated by cuttings and by seed

To the botanists who divide *Pelargonium* species into fifteen sections, horticulturalists who divide them into five, and nurserymen who use whatever method best suits their catalogues, it is galling that the general public refers to almost all the plants as 'Geraniums' and has done so for at least 400 years. To set the matter straight, there are two genera *Geranium* and *Pelargonium* that are quite distinct but, because they have fruits like a bird's beak, they belong to the same botanic family. The former is named from the Greek for crane, the latter from the Greek for stork. Moreoever, few people actually grow *Geranium* species, but *Pelargonium* species are exceptionally popular. There are nurseries that trade in nothing else; hybridists who devote their whole lives to producing finer cultivars, all descendants of the 250 or so species of *Pelargonium* brought to Europe from South Africa in the 1770s, and others found later in Madagascar, Arabia, West India, and Australia. The zeal of the old florists has somehow communicated itself to the Pelargonium fanciers of today and undoubtedly they are ideal plants for the small greenhouse or garden room. By taking batches of 5-centimetre (2-inch) cuttings three times a year and potting into 12-centimetre (5-inch) pots, a collection will be in blossom twelve months out of twelve, at a very modest cost. It is scarcely surprising that they have a wide appeal though, unfortunately, like racehorses and roses, some of the best cultivars have been given unlovely names such as Confetti, All my Love, Twinkle, and Grand Slam.

The species figured was considered remarkable because of the lanceolate shape of the leaves. To collectors its foliage has the added attraction of being grey-green and sometimes mealy like the leaves of an Auricula. To the plant historian it is an excellent example of fortuitous introduction. A very important 18th century London gardener was James Lee, first an employee of the Duke of Northumberland, then a nurseryman at Hammersmith in partnership with a Mr Lewis Kennedy. Both were acquainted with Sir Joseph Banks and both had the privilege of using his library and examining herbarium material as it came in. Looking over a packet of dried plants sent from the Cape, Lee judged that two or three of the seeds might still be viable. He begged to be allowed to try and germinate them. His success resulted in this modest Pelargonium becoming available to gardeners from 1775.

31.

Plate 83

Pelargonium glaucum

Ixia viridiflora Lam.

GREEN IXIA

FAMILY: Iridaceae
SYNONYM: *Ixia maculata* L. var. *viridis*
DISTRIBUTION: South Africa: Cape Province
CULTIVATION: half-hardy corm; in cold regions the corms are better lifted in winter; propagated by corm offsets or by seed; numerous hybrids and garden varieties

ACCORDING to a book on edible plants published in 1783 the corms of *Ixia* species were regularly eaten by the natives of South Africa. This might account for the unhappy rarity of the species found by Thunberg many days' journey from the Cape which he named *I. viridiflora* and introduced into cultivation before he journeyed on to the Far East in 1775. Its success was ensured by a Dr Fothergill whose name appears constantly in the botanical papers of the day. This gentleman has been called 'obstinate and litigatious' but his skill as a physician in fashionable London brought him a great fortune which he used for the furthering of scientific knowledge. He was a friend of Joseph Banks and Benjamin Franklin and had enormous collections of dried insects and shells, but these came second to his love for plants. He bought an estate and made it into a large botanic garden that Banks claimed was second only to Kew, and, being a perfectionist, Fothergill was not content with ephemeral growing plants or with dried herbarium specimens, but employed a number of artists to figure plants as they were sent to him from all over the world.[1] Not being quite hardy all Ixias presented a problem to the Doctor which he instantly mastered by determining they were pot plants, and it was as pot plants they were grown in cultivation for many, many years. It would seem that Thunberg and Fothergill between them saved this green Ixia from extinction. If it is now found in the wild it should be left severely alone. Corms can be bought as it is one of the few Ixia species to survive in nurserymen's lists. The other Ixias offered are generally hardy cultivars of mixed strains and great colour variations. *I. viridiflora* is frequently described as being 'unreal' or 'more like an artificial plant', its colouring as 'a pale turquoise', 'electric greenish-blue', but the truth seems to be that the intensity and shade of green differs from flower to flower. This startling colour contrasted with the black eye at the centre and the patterns of the three conspicuous stamens make it one of the most exciting of Cape flowering plants. Its petals are as delicate as those of a Poppy or Cistus and, because of this, the bright colouring is observable when the flower is closed and they even preserve their beauty when carefully pressed and dried. It does not matter then that the genus is shy of clouds and the flowers close when the sun is covered, for it can still be enjoyed.

[1] At his death 1200 natural history drawings were bought from his estate for Catherine the Great, Empress of Russia.

Plate 84

Ixia viridiflora

Hebe elliptica (Forst. fil.) Pennell

FAMILY: Scrophulariaceae
SYNONYMS: *Veronica elliptica* Forst. fil., *V. decussata* Sol.
DISTRIBUTION: New Zealand, Falkland Islands, Tierra del Fuego, and South America
north to lat. 45° 53′S.
CULTIVATION: half-hardy, bushy, evergreen shrub; it withstands some frost but needs
a sheltered position or it can be brought into a cool greenhouse over winter; propagated
by cuttings

THE irascible Dr Fothergill was sent this plant in 1776 from the far-distant Falkland
Islands, then botanically lean with less than 120 flowering plants on all the islands,
doubtless on account of the suddenly changing temperature and humidity. Who had
the honour of despatching the first seeds to Europe remains unknown because
Fothergill's Botanic Garden fell into desuetude, to be ultimately gulped up into
Greater London, and such records were lost; but by using the resources at his disposal
the Doctor may be attributed with its introduction into cultivation. Hebes belong to
the Veronicas or Speedwells, a genus within the Figwort family of plants and they are
often considered a sub-genus because of slight botanical differences. It also happens
that they have their provenance in the Southern hemisphere whereas the other pair of
Veronica sub-genera come from the north. The distribution of *H. elliptica* is important
so far as the past history and pre-history of Antarctica are concerned for it connects
New Zealand with South America and the neighbouring continental islands, but has
not jumped that thousand miles of profoundly deep water to Botany Bay in the north-
east. It is the largest of all Hebes, growing to 7 metres (20 feet), and being salt-
resistant and evergreen it must have been of inestimable value in the windswept
Falkland Islands where for a long time there were no trees to speak of and the settlers
were in desperate need of shelter belts and timber. The flowers are proportionately
large, between four and twelve of them on every raceme, each 1.6 centimetres (0.6
inches) across, and they are not quire at the end of a branch. Besides being attractive
they are also deliciously scented and fertilizing insects also enjoy the fragrance and the
promise that it carries of nectar. They land on a petal edge to get at the honey and grasp
the two stamens to support themselves. This swings the anthers down on to their back
to give them a thorough dusting of pollen.

A modern hybrid named Autumn Glory that is less rampageous and has many
fragrant purple flowers with yellow anthers is some sort of distant relation. A closer
one is *H.* × *franciscana* 'Latifolia', the most common of all Hebes, that has blue-mauve
flowers with a fine scent, and makes a conical-shaped bush or can be used for thick
hedging.

Plate 85

Hebe elliptica

Alstromeria caryophyllaea Jacq.

STRIPED ALSTROMERIA

FAMILY: Alstromeriaceae (Amaryllidaceae)
SYNONYM: *Alstromeria ligtu* sensu Bot. Mag.
DISTRIBUTION: Brazil
CULTIVATION: non-hardy perennial; a plant for the stove or warm house; propagated by seed or by dividing the roots

CLAES Alstroemer was a disciple of Linnaeus honoured not only by a genus *Alstromeria* but, according to one system of classification last brought up to date in 1973, by a plant family Alstromeriaceae which has four genera. In fact he did little to win immortality. Very sensibly he collected in Spain where the botanical treasure of the Spanish Americas made it a plantsman's Eldorado. There he found the Chilean plant named after him, *A. pelegrina*, and sent several of the fleshy roots to Sweden. The delighted Linnaeus had the plants put in his bedroom at night time to protect them from the cold. In full growth they proved to have been worth his care: a head of flowers on a long stem coloured lilac with a striped exterior and yellow and purple markings. This was in 1754. A few years later, in 1776, a Mr John Brown introduced the species shown in the plate.

A. caryophyllaea was variously reported as having been found on riversides in Chile and as a native of Peru. In fact its original home was Brazil. It was greatly admired for its striped, fiery red blossoms and for its fragrance said to be scarcely inferior to Mignonette which at that time put it in a very high class indeed. Moreover, it had a curiosity value as the only garden plant with upside-down leaves caused by a twist in the stalk, and for its fruit capsules that exploded prodigiously scattering seeds like shot from a gun. As, supposedly, they needed protection, Alstromerias were at first grown exclusively as stove plants, then in cool greenhouses. And undoubtedly they do do well in pots so long as they are staked and kept moist all the time their roots are working. Even after blooming and the leaves and flowers are dead the roots must be prevented from shrivelling up with an occasional douse. However, the hardier species – which does not include *A. caryophyllaea* – can be grown out of doors so long as they are planted deeply. This presented a problem because it seemed they resented deep planting. Then some unknown garden benefactor solved it. He scooped out a hole, 30 centimetres (a foot) deep, laid the Alstromerias in the bottom, and scarcely covered the roots. As the crowns sprouted he filled the hole in little by little until the leaf and flower stems were held secure by 30 centimetres of good loam.

Plate 86

Alstromeria caryophyllaea

Senecio cruentus (Masson) DC.

PURPLE-LEAVED CINERARIA

FAMILY: Compositae
SYNONYM: *Cineraria cruenta* Masson, *C. hybrida* hort.
DISTRIBUTION: northern part of Tenerife, Canary Islands
CULTIVATION: non-hardy perennial; a coolhouse plant that needs high air humidity and partial shade; propagated by cuttings or by seed

THIS cousin of the Ragworts, Fleaworts, and Common Groundsel was found by Masson in the Canary Islands in 1777. Some species of *Senecio* have inconspicuous flowers because they pollinate themselves. The majority, including Masson's find, have blossoms that look simple but really are rather complicated. What appear to be 'flowers' arranged in a loose cluster are in fact compound flower-heads. The 'petals' are themselves small asymmetric ray-flowers arranged round a disk of tightly packed, symmetric flowers. The arrangement virtually guarantees fertilization and widespread seeding because the cluster ensures the maximum attraction to pollinating insects, and the mass of flowers packed closely together ensures that most are fertilized by one insect in one visit. This is of particular interest to the botanist. The gardener is equally interested in the great variations of shape, texture, and colour of the foliage but less so in the flower as the predominant colours are yellow and mauve in different shades and degrees of dinginess. Therefore the introduction of Canary Island species that showed traces of red was something of an event. *S. populifolius*, introduced anonymously at no recorded date, had ray-flowers of pink or purple. *S. heritieri*, introduced by and named for a French collector in 1774, had ray-flowers of white and pink or crimson. Masson's introduction of three years later with its deep lilac disk-flowers and ray-flowers of purplish-red was the third and ultimately the most successful of all. Hybridists went to work, crossing and re-crossing the three species backwards and forwards; but it was from crossing different plants of *S. cruentus* that the most remarkable result occurred. In time there evolved a stablized and entirely new herbaceous woody plant grown as an annual for decorating greenhouses and conservatories and windowsills, that brought a new source of gold to the nursery trade, the garden Cineraria. Between them international experts have produced a large range of cultivars, divided into six specific types and of all colours, blues, reds, pinks, and whites. The lurid market plants of fifty years ago are slowly giving way to those with more subtle shades and colour combinations. How far a cry it is from Masson's plant that was once said to be particularly brilliant in candlelight to the most frequently sold pot plant in the Western world.

Plate 87

Senecio cruentus

Calceolaria fothergillii Sol.

FOTHERGILL'S SLIPPER WORT

FAMILY: Scrophulariaceae
DISTRIBUTION: South America, Patagonia, and Falkland Islands
CULTIVATION: half-hardy, creeping perennial; it requires moist, humus-rich soil and partial shade, it does not withstand severe frosts and should be covered or brought into a cool greenhouse in winter; propagated by seed or, with care, by cuttings

THOUGH it has so close a relative in the genus *Jovellana*[1] that proves some sort of connection between New Zealand and South America, the genus *Calceolaria*, named from the Greek word for shoe, is exclusive to Central and South America. It belongs to one of the largest of all genera, and there is a huge number of species, some of great beauty, but most remain listed in encyclopaedias instead of being grown as lovely annuals out of doors or as equally lovely dwarf perennials in rock gardens. Virtually the only Calceolarias we see in the last quarter of the 20th century are grown either as forced pot plants or as shrubby perennials for bedding out, and, while there are a number of daintily pouched and coloured cultivars, there are also many that have had their slippers bloated out to clogs and in the mass appear rather blowsy. Only a few discerning alpine gardeners are the proud owners of such small species as *C. volkmannii* from Chile, *C. scapiflora* from Peru, *C. darwinii* from the Straits of Magellan, *C. polyrrhiza* from Patagonia, and Dr Fothergill's Slipperwort that he imported from the Falkland Islands in 1777. It seems extraordinary that such an exotic flower should belong to the pauciflorous, storm-wracked, ocean-bound archipelago where the climate was far kinder to penguins than to plants or men. It seems equally surprising that at first it proved so difficult to cultivate. Its native home, subject to fierce gales and to the icy fingers of the Cape Horn and South Atlantic currents, ensured the plant's hardiness to some cold. Yet it began to fail and several times was given up for lost. Possibly it was coddled, or given too much water about the roots. By luck it adapted itself to Europe and survived. The curious flower on its hairy pink stalk might be said to look like an opulent shoe, perhaps for a caliph, though surely for ceremonial rather than practical purposes. The coloured engraving suggests something else: a throne elevated above a conglomeration of bottle-green leaves, and no simple throne but a seat and back of mahogany and gold with a small cream cushion, and a canopy of gold and white and green. It might be a flower of that strange plant figured by Edward Lear in his *Laughable Lyrics* of a hundred years ago, *Armchairia comfortabilis*.

[1] The botanical distinction is small. In appearance the two lips of *Jovellana* are never shoe-shaped.

Plate 88

Calceolaria fothergillii

Dianthus caryophyllus L. 'Franklin's Tartar'

BIZARRE BORDER CARNATION

FAMILY: Caryophyllaceae
CULTIVATION: perennial with hardy and non-hardy varieties; cultivation depends
largely on the variety and the grower; propagated by stem cuttings or layering

IT has been remarked before in this volume that there is a world of difference between the old-fashioned florists and the modern shopkeeper who sells cut flowers and house-plants. The former belonged to a very special class, all male, mostly of humble origin, usually craftsmen or artisans, and possessed of a strong competitive spirit, a strict regard for the properties of a flower or fruit or vegetable, and a relish for raising champions. The first florists were immigrants to England, generally weavers from France and the Low Countries, who took their garden treasures with them. Men spent all they could afford, and sometimes more, on breeding plants for competition and pocket-handkerchief-sized gardens, back yards, greenhouses knocked together with bits and pieces, even protected window boxes produced champions that would have done honour to the head gardener of a great establishment with every facility at his disposal. The Carnation was generally regarded as the apogee of artisans' flowers and these were the Border Carnations which had steadily been improved from the days when Parksinson listed varieties with the charming names of Red Hello and Blue Hello and The Greatest Granado. By the end of the 18th century three kinds of show flowers had evolved: Bizarres, Flakes, and Picotees. The scarlet Carnation with strong black and white markings shown in the plate is a splendid Bizarre. The date it was raised by Mr Franklin is unknown and 1778 is arbitrarily chosen simply because he was then cultivating Carnations in Lambeth Marsh where William Curtis had his first Botanic Garden. Each cultivator and breeder had his secret tricks but it was the general practice to use a compost of light sandy loam mixed in equal quantities with well-rotted and dried horse or cow dung that had been sun-roasted to eliminate grubs and especially the dangerous Carnation Maggot. After that the plant was gorged on the right quantity and no more of liquid manure, a favourite being made from sheep's dung. It is a melancholy aspect of improvement that favourites are lost or pushed aside by replacements. Border Carnations are now divided into six different types, Selfs and Fancies having been added. But Franklin's Tartar and scores of other beauties have sadly followed John Parkinson's Red Hello, Blue Hello, and The Greatest Granado into oblivion.

Plate 89

Dianthus caryophyllus

Salvia leonuroides Gloxin

SHINING SAGE

FAMILY: Labiatae
SYNONYMS: *Salvia formosa* L'Hérit., *S. nodosa* R. & P.
DISTRIBUTION: Peru and Ecuador
CULTIVATION: non-hardy perennial; better kept in a cool greenhouse but it can be
planted out in summer; propagated by cuttings

IT is extraordinary how certain plants enjoy a vogue that dies down and, after a period, flares up again. The Sages or Salvias have experienced just such capricious attention; made much of at the beginning of the last century, allowed to slip out of fashion for a hundred years, then being brought back with a certain degree of enthusiasm. Some of the annual species, or those grown as such, especially the Scarlet Sage, *S. splendens*, with all its cultivars, have become the darlings of municipal and institutional gardeners and consequently objects of loathing to those who dislike bedding-out schemes and any sort of horticultural regimentation. There are, however, greenhouse species that are useful foils to other plants, especially to Chrysanthemums in the autumn. The genus is vast. It has between 700 and 900 species yet probably less than 120 are in cultivation, and it is doubtful if more than 30 greenhouse species are obtainable. Of these 30, 12 have the special merit of blooming in autumn or winter; one yellow species, two purple, two blue, and the remainder different shades of red. But most have become rarities. Certainly the Shining Sage figured in the plate is now virtually extinct in cultivation which is odd considering it was so highly thought of at the time of its introduction from Peru in 1783 because it was one of the very few species with flowers neatly growing from its leaf axils.

Pliny gave the genus its name from the Latin *salvere* to be in good health, and doubtless the Shining Sage shares some of the properties attributed to the Garden Sage that combines with Onion as the perfect palate baffle for greasy meats; makes excellent tea and beer; and is a panacea to Mother Nature healers unless it is over used which leads to hideous discomfort and even convulsions. All species secrete volatile oils and have bitter principles and characteristic scents. Should anyone be the fortunate possessor of a Shining Sage let him bruise a flower or one of those handsomely shaped, leathery leaves with smooth uppersides and a matted mass of hairs below, and the air about him will at once be redolent of Clary, a singular smell used in quality scents and a secret flavouring ingredient of many vermouths.

Plate 90

Salvia leonuroides

Eucomis punctata (Thunb.) L'Hérit.

SPOTTED-LEAVED EUCOMIS

FAMILY: Liliaceae
SYNONYM: *Eucomis comosa* hort.
DISTRIBUTION: South Africa
CULTIVATION: non-hardy bulb; it makes a good pot plant for a cool greenhouse or it may be grown as a house-plant; propagated by bulb offsets or by seed

A MUCH respected gardener named John Graefer was responsible for the introduction of *Eucomis punctata* from the Cape in 1783. Doubtless earlier introductions had failed for both Thunberg and Masson wrote the plant up, but the honour of bringing it into general cultivation belongs to Graefer. He was a London nurseryman, celebrated for his method of drying green vegetables, an invention siezed on by the Admiralty in the need to keep down scurvy in the Royal Navy, and for the publication of a most useful catalogue of plants with details about their provenance, requirements, colour, and height. On the recommendation of Sir Joseph Banks – who inevitably by then had been made a baronet for his services to science and firmly had his finger in the pie of such appointments – Graefer became Gardener to that remarkable woman Queen Maria-Carolina, consort of Ferdinand IV, the King of the Two Sicilies, a genial monarch who caught and sold fish to his Neapolitan subjects and was affectionately known by them as Big Nose. Later when Nelson was given the Dukedom of Bronté, Graefer became his resident steward. His rise in fortune had been steady but he found the nurture of exotics more palatable than managing a Sicilian estate for an absentee landlord, and certainly easier for he was not a particularly good steward. Nelson recorded his death at Bronté on 7 August 1802. He is remembered by plantsmen in this *Eucomis* called variously *punctata* from the spots of purple at the base of the stem and on the leaves, or *comosa* on account of the tuft of leaf-like bracts on top of the flower spike that bears so close a resemblance to a pineapple. The clever design of the plate indicates its size. It is a large plant that grows from a big egg-shaped bulb to a height of a metre (3 feet); and the grooved leaves with a slight wave to the edge are lance-shaped and 60 centimetres (2 feet) long. Their green colour suggests the shade of a billiard table cloth and brings out the green in the flowers. These vary considerably in colour from yellowy-green to white touched with rose pink or claret which with the wine-coloured ovary makes them very desirable as cut flowers. Alone in the genus this species has a fragrance, and as they are good to look at from the time the fresh green leaves begin to emerge from the bulb until well into the fruiting stage they give months of pleasure.

Plate 91

Eucomis punctata

Aloysia triphylla (L'Hérit.) Britton

LEMON VERBENA

FAMILY: Verbenaceae

SYNONYMS: *Verbena triphylla* L'Hérit., *Aloysia citriodora* Ort., *Lippia citriodora* (Ort.) H.B.K.

DISTRIBUTION: West Indies and warmer parts of America, naturalized elsewhere

CULTIVATION: half-hardy shrub or small tree; it requires protection from frost or it can be grown in a cool greenhouse; propagated by cuttings

THE Lemon Verbena came originally from Argentina and Chile where it grows to a height of 7 metres (20 feet) and the oil is collected for the scent industry and other purposes. The aroma lies chiefly in the glands of the leaves that are arranged in trios round the stem. Either fresh or dried they exude a strong scent of lemon. The trumpet flowers of white or lilac are insignificant but have something to be said for them if they are examined through a hand glass. The plant was introduced anonymously from South America, passing through the hands of Spanish and French botanists, but it was not widely grown until after 1784 when John Sibthorpe saw a plant in Paris and decided it deserved wide appreciation. His recommendations were a spur to its recognition as a popular garden shrub and therefore he may be said to be its impresario if not its introducer into cultivation. Few plants have been promoted by such a colourful personality. His father was Professor of Botany at Oxford for thirty-six years, during which time he delivered only one lecture and that was notably dull,[1] and he passed on his Professorial Chair to John. Nepotism then was considered a perfectly respectable and natural way of caring for one's own. The new Professor, aged 25, promptly turned over the work to a deputy and left for Greece intent on finding all the 600 plants described by Dioscorides. He made two expeditions. On the first he botanised undaunted by the threat of local wars, rebellions, and an outbreak of plague. On the second journey he was accompanied by an Italian, Francesco Boroni. They were struck down with fever at Constantinople, recovered, climbed Olympus botanising up to the summit, and only just escaped being captured by Barbary pirates. Then, at Athens, Boroni fell asleep in an upper window, toppled out, and broke his neck.[2] Sibthorpe was much afflicted but he quickly hired another collector and went on working until he fell ill a second time in the ruins of Nicopolis and struggled back to Oxford to die, aged only 36. His ambitious work was not published for years. His vast and valuable correspondence was stored by a sister and after her death was burnt on a bonfire as rubbish.

[1] Yet he was of sufficient standing for Linnaeus to name after him the genus *Sibthorpia*.

[2] The Italian was immortalized in the genus of Australian evergreen shrub, *Boronia*.

Plate 92

Aloysia triphylla

Centropogon cornutus (L.) Druce

FAMILY: Campanulaceae (Lobeliaceae)
SYNONYMS: *Lobelia cornuta* L., *L. surinamensis* L., *Centropogon surinamensis* (L.) Presl.
DISTRIBUTION: Central and South America
CULTIVATION: non-hardy sub-shrub; it requires a warm greenhouse and moist soil, it flowers during the winter but while flowering it should not be kept too wet; propagated by cuttings

THE great plant family of Campanulaceae or Bellflowers is divided by some botanists into sub-divisions: the genus figured here falling in the Lobeliaceae that have flowers which are generally symmetric on one plane, like that of a Deadnettle or Foxglove, and with their anthers united so that the stamens form a little tube as happens in the Dandelion family. The Lobeliaceae family both fascinates and torments botanists because it poses some as yet unanswerable questions about the evolution of plants. For example, it has six genera of trees, four of them growing only on the Hawaiian Islands that are geographically remote and geologically young. Then there is a shrubby species as totally isolated on the island of St Helena as Napoleon was in exile. And the figured genus *Centropogon*, has a relative *Siphocampylus* from which it differs in the smallest botanical particulars and both are found only in Tropical America. The Lobeliaceae is also remarkable in the amazing variety of plant growth that falls within it. There is the tiny plant used for edging and as a trailer so familiar to gardeners, and there are grotesque giants from the high mountains of Africa, four to five times the height of a man, that, as much as anything, resemble dressed-up totem poles. Species of *Centropogon* also vary from one another. Some are upstanding branched shrubs, a metre (3 feet) high; others lie on the ground and are used in hanging baskets. Therefore the subject of Sydenham Edwards's exquisitely arranged drawing, in which the flowers appear to bow to one another, belongs to a very intriguing part of the Bellflower family. Notice that the bells do not hang. To use a term used by English bellringers, they have been 'fetched up'. The clappers are the united anthers which have hairs, a feature that gave the genus its name from the Greek for spur and beard. It is endemic to South and Central America and the West Indies whence it was first sent to Europe in 1786, a year that seemed to hinge two alien worlds for in it uranium was discovered, Mont Blanc conquered, and gas lighting was first tried in England and Germany, while at Potsdam, Frederick the Great finally gave way to a lifetime's onslaught of ill health and died.

Plate 93

Centropogon cornutus

Maurandya scandens Pers.

BASTARD FOXGLOVE

FAMILY: Scrophulariaceae
SYNONYM: *Maurandya semperflorens* Ort.
DISTRIBUTION: Mexico
CULTIVATION: non-hardy perennial or annual climber; it can be grown out of doors as an annual or kept in a cool greenhouse as a perennial; propagated by seed or by cuttings

SEEDS of this Mexican plant were sent to the botanical headquarters of the Spanish Empire in Madrid where Dr Casimiro Gómez de Ortega grew them successfully in the Royal Gardens and he in turn was able to distribute seeds through Europe about the year 1786. Ultimately, and for no known reason, it was named for Señora Catherine Maurandy, a botanist at the Botanical Gardens in Cartagena. It is another member of the Figwort family that is particularly generous to gardeners providing as it does among dozens of other favourites, Foxgloves, Snapdragons, Penstemons, Mulleins, and Monkey Flowers. William Curtis named the Maurandya Bastard Foxglove as its flower bears some resemblance to the wild flower, but it was one of his contrived names and the plant really has no common name. Its petals are joined to form a frilly edged tube that encloses four stamens and is comfortably adapted for the visits of pollinators. A majority of the ten species in the genus have purple flowers, marked and veined both inside and outside the tube; but to many the main beauty of the plant lies in the foliage: small but bold leaves shaped like arrow-heads and of a bright lettuce-green with sensitive stalks.

Climbers climb because they want to move towards light and they use a support in different ways. Some, like Hops and Honeysuckle, have a twining stem that grows in a spiral and, once it touches a host, it winds round it, continuing its growth as it climbs higher. Miraculously the stem is only induced to twine by the right contact. Wind pressure or heavy rain or other possible stimulants have no effect at all. In other words, it appears to know what to climb up. Other plants sprawl over their hosts by means of prickles, such as the Blackberry and Rose. Others like Ivy are specially equipped with stem roots to dig and anchor into crevices. Others such as Virginia Creeper have suction pads. But the principal method of climbing is undoubtedly by means of tendrils. Either they are modified stems or shoots like the spring-coil tendrils of a Cucumber, or they are leaf tendrils like those of Sweet Peas. Maurandyas have a most unusual way of hoisting themselves. It is their leaf stalks that are stimulated. At a touch they immediately wrap themselves round a host, and, if the conditions are right, they can cover a wooden lattice at a phenomenal speed.

Plate 94

Maurandya scandens

Kalmia hirsuta Walter

HAIRY MOUNTAIN LAUREL

FAMILY: Ericaceae
DISTRIBUTION: south-eastern USA
CULTIVATION: half-hardy, small evergreen shrub; it requires moist, lime-free soil and protection from frost, it is difficult to cultivate in Europe and has virtually disappeared from plant catalogues; propagated by cuttings, layers, or seed

THREE important people were connected with the introduction of this charming Kalmia. The first was William Aiton, Royal Gardener at Kew, who looked after the collections there for thirty-six years and made a notable contribution to science by listing and detailing them in his *Hortus Kewensis*. The second was Sir James Smith, a specialist in Willows, who three years after the death of Linnaeus carried off the scientific scoop of the century by buying his herbarium, library, and effects,[1] and founded the Linnean Society that thrives strongly to the present day. The third person who actually collected and introduced the Kalmia was a Scot named John Fraser. He began life as a draper but plants proved to be an irresistible lure and he cut himself loose from his trade, accepted the patronage of Aiton and Smith, and sailed for America. Between 1780 and the turn of the century he crossed the Atlantic a dozen times latterly accompanied by his son, another John, and between them they introduced scores of trees and shrubs chiefly from the south-eastern colonies, apparently oblivious of the war between the British and the rebel colonials that raged about them or any of the great political events of the era. To them plants mattered more. It is sad to note that after such service to science Fraser senior fell into debt and died a ruined man.

Kalmias are a small group of shrubs the roots of which have been used for the bowls of tobacco pipes and the manufacture of spoons. The plant is poisonous and, traditionally, if an old Red Indian felt it was time to move to happier hunting grounds he would stoically chew the leaves until he achieved his object. *K. hirsuta* is a very distinct species on account of its hairiness and the fact that it grows upright and its flowers are not in terminal clusters. The flowers have an artful pollinating mechanism. The inside of the corolla resembles a parasol with its ten ribs bent the wrong way. These ribs are really tautly bent stamen filaments, their anthers held lightly by the edge of the corolla, but with the precision of a well-set mouse trap. Any honey-hungry insect that merely brushes a filament will move the anther and the whole stamen swings back to dust the intruder with pollen or pollinate its own stigma.

[1] They included the rhinoceros-horn drinking cup given by Lagerstroem to Linnaeus alleged to detect poisons and increase potency. It would appear that it also carried the gift of long life. Linnaeus died at 71, a respectable age in the 18th century. Sir James Smith died at 69. Lady Smith died at 104. The Linnean Society with a keen sense of what was fitting presented it to the King of Sweden in 1970 on his eighty-eighth birthday and he died in his ninety-first year.

Plate 95

Kalmia hirsuta

Epidendrum cochleatum L.

PURPLE-FLOWERED EPIDENDRUM, CLAM FLOWER

FAMILY: Orchidaceae
DISTRIBUTION: Central America and West Indies
CULTIVATION: perennial epiphyte; it requires a heated greenhouse and grows in a
fibrous substrate such as tree bark, royal or tree fern stems; propagated by division

THIS particular Orchid was introduced to Europe from the West Indies in 1786 and
was said to be the first of its kind to flower in England. It heralded an interest in the
order that grew in the high noon of 19th century plant-hunting to what appeared
nothing less than madness among collectors. The Orchid became a symbol of luxury
and beauty. Fables circulated that amongst the genera there were parasites that fed on
other plants, monsters that consumed human flesh, sovereign remedies for disease and
impotency, and that all Orchids were as delicate as they were rare. Eventually these
myths were scotched, but even discounting them Orchids still remain extraordinary.
Their fruits contain thousands, even millions of tiny wind-borne seeds because, unlike
other seeds, they contain nothing to sustain their growth and so must feed on a species
of fungus. Hence their prodigal seeding. They vary enormously in size from plants no
bigger than a snailshell to giants that can scramble to 33 metres (100 feet), and they
vary as much in type. Some have no leaves and pop up spontaneously from the ground.
Some live in water, some in deserts, some in grassland. Some, like this Epidendrum,
perch like birds in trees. Botanically they are unique, having their male and female
parts contained together in a column rather than in the more usual separate
arrangement but they will only fertilize themselves as a last resort and are designed in
many cunning ways to ensure they shall be fertilized by insects. It is another feature of
Orchids that pollen grains are massed together into pollinia.[1] In Epidendrums they are
waxy little blobs. The plate shows another characteristic of many tree-perching species
that drop their leaves in the dry season. The onion-shaped stem is not a true bulb but a
store for water and other reserves. These stores grow annually. Moreover, it has three
distinct kinds of root; one, insensitive both to gravity and the pull of the sun, clings to
the support; another is for absorbing food from humus that settles between the plant
and its support and can and does move in any direction; and the last is a true aerial root
that hangs in a festoon and takes in moisture.

[1] The only exceptions in the 17,000-odd species of Orchid are those in the Apostasioïdeae and the
Cypripedioïeae.

196

Plate 96

Epidendrum cochleatum

Nymphaea odorata Ait.

SWEET-SCENTED WATER-LILY

FAMILY: Nymphaeaceae
DISTRIBUTION: eastern North America from Nova Scotia to Arkansas
CULTIVATION: aquatic perennial; although often treated as non-hardy, the wild species
is very hardy and very adaptable, growing equally well in deep or shallow water;
propagated by seed or by division of the rhizome; the flowers close at midday

WATER-LILIES have an illustrious history. At the lowest level their seeds and tubers have been regularly eaten and used for dyeing and in the preparation of beer. At a higher level, Theophrastus and, after him, Dioscorides included species in their lists of healing plants, and a chemical analysis of the fleshy rhizomes reveals they contain amongst other things tannin, starch, sugar, gum, resin, ammonia, tartaric and gallic acids, and a vegetable gelatine composed of carbon, hydrogen, and oxygen. At the same practical level it is suggested that the furled sepals furnished the Greeks with the basic idea for the Ionic capital and this led to other architectural ornamental features. At the highest level their symmetry and purity made both orientals and occidentals regard them as symbols of men's best aspirations and consider them a quasi-sacred plant. In the gardens of the Near East, Moorish Spain, Italy, and France they held supreme place; though not in England where for a long time water gardens were disliked. 'Pools mar all,' wrote Francis Bacon, 'and make the garden unwholesome and full of flies and frogs'. Nevertheless it was through England that Europe received the plant figured here from North America in 1786. Like the common *N. alba* it was a deep-water aquatic and at first sight it also looked much the same. But there were small differences. Beneath the leaves of the American plant there were prominent veins; the white flowers were slightly flushed with red; above all it was fragrant. It became a great favourite in the Old World even converting some English gardeners from their insular prejudice, and then, by a freak of fortune, a fresh American variety was found that finally established its popularity. More than a hundred years after the first introduction of *N. odorata* a farmer in West Virginia turned up some Water-lily tubers with his ploughshare in a low-lying piece of land. Evidently there had once been a pond there long since filled in. He planted some out. The flowers were deep pink and had the same delightful scent. Those plough-turned tubers were the progenitors of thousands that spread through the water gardens of the world. And they are still esteemed even though, owing to the genius of a French hybridist, M. Josef Bory Latour-Marliac, the modern grower has Water-lilies of many different colours and size from which to choose.

Plate 97

Nymphaea odorata

Nelumbo nucifera Gaertn.

SACRED LOTUS, BEAN OF INDIA

FAMILY: Nelumbonaceae (Nymphaeaceae)
SYNONYM: *Nelumbium speciosum* Willd.
DISTRIBUTION: Persia, India, South and South-east Asia, Australia, naturalized elsewhere
CULTIVATION: non-hardy, aquatic perennial; it requires a lot of space and a well-manured soil, it can be planted outdoors in summer; propagated by division of the rhizome or by seed

MENTION was made in the notes on *Nymphaea odorata* that the Water-lily was regarded as a quasi-sacred plant. The *Nelumbo* is not a *Nymphaea* nor even closely related, but it bears some resemblance, and is most certainly regarded as holy, being the Sacred Lotus, introduced to Egypt about 500 BC where it was believed to contain the secrets of the gods and in particular was consecrated to the sun. The Pharoanic Egyptians both worshipped the Lotus and worshipped with it, offering the flowers upon their altars. It no longer grows beside the Nile but is venerated in all countries to the East for its association with creation, preservation, the afterlife, ultimate beauty, and holiness. It appears in the structure of temple buildings, in decorations, invariably as part of sacred images, and in the prayers and songs and literature of millions of devout people from Syria where the Lotus symbolizes the cradle of Moses, to high Tibet where the prayer wheels whirl endlessly repeating the word as an essential part of Lama worship, through India and Indonesia to China and Japan. It is unlikely that this plant should have achieved such a position in the thought and religion of so many people simply because it happens to be beautiful or because its parts suggest symbols of devotional value. A more likely reason is because of its singularity. Nelumbonaceae is one of about 500 major plant families that are subdivided into genera and species that make up an estimated 225,000 flowering plants. But within Nelumbonaceae there is only one genus, *Nelumbo,* and this genus has only two species: one with yellow flowers from America and the Sacred Lotus that now spreads on the map in the shape of a poached egg from the Caspian Sea to North Australia and New Guinea at the bottom of the egg to the Sea of Japan at its crown.[1] Moreover, it has a peculiar leaf arrangement that, botanically, is unique. It is improbable that most people are aware of these marks of singularity which heightens the mystery that so extraordinary a plant in all respects should be counted important in three of the world's great religions. To Sir Joseph Banks, through whose patronage it was brought to grow in European stoves in 1787, its waxy leaves, fragrant flowers, and fruiting heads resembling the rose of a watering pot, would have been subjects of great fascination, but he could hardly have guessed that to virtually half the world's population it was the most important of all plants.

---

[1] Fossils reveal that millions of years ago it grew in Upper Egypt, Portugal, and Holland, and in a crescent-shaped mass that spread from the south of England through France, Switzerland, Austria, and Hungary as far east as the Ukraine.

Erica ventricosa Thunb.

PORCELAIN HEATH

FAMILY: Ericaceae
DISTRIBUTION: South Africa: Cape Province
CULTIVATION: non-hardy, compact shrub; suitable for a cool greenhouse, it requires a
loose, lime-free potting mixture; propagated by cuttings

IN the first twenty-five bound volumes of the *Botanical Magazine* there are many
plates of Heaths. This is partly because a majority, and certainly the most obviously
decorative of the 500 species of *Erica*, come from South Africa which was then being
intensely if not systematically explored by botanists and gardeners, and it was also due
to William Curtis's friendship with a nurseryman who specialized in Heaths and did
much to popularize them. Conrad Loddiges was an Hanoverian who in 1783 had leased
land in Hackney and built up an enviable reputation as a gardener. His nursery was
acknowledged as '*remarkable for orderly arrangement and for the magnitude and the extent of
the hot-houses*', and when William Curtis moved his Botanic Garden to Brompton in
1790 Loddiges was amongst the many friends and admirers who helped the enterprise
with contributions of plants. Doubtless many of them were Heaths. The Porcelain
Heath is a good representative of Cape Heaths and has the advantage over most of the
others in that it is still in cultivation. It is doubtful if many of the other early
introductions are now available. At the beginning of the last century more than 180
species were being grown at Kew but they were mostly displaced and many that were
commonplace a hundred years ago are now lost. Curtis's name Porcelain Heath suits
this species well. Shaped like little jars, the corollas of the palest pink have a finished,
glazed look as though they are made of porcelain, and are nipped at the neck. The
flowering season is long and the plants bloom in the northern hemisphere as they do in
the southern from May to September. The species was first brought into cultivation in
1787. Masson, on a second tour of duty at the Cape, found specimens of 1.8 metres
(6 feet) growing at a high altitude in the mountains, and was responsible for its
introduction. Thunberg described and named it.

Nelumbo nucifera

Plate 98

Plate 99

Erica ventricosa

Calopogon pulchellus (Salisb.) R. Br.

PRETTY CALOPOGON, GRASS-PINK

FAMILY: Orchidaceae
SYNONYM: *Limodorum tuberosum* sensu Bot. Mag.
DISTRIBUTION: eastern North America from Newfoundland to Florida, Bahamas and
Cuba
CULTIVATION: tuberous-rooted perennial; it is a variable species, some races are hardy
others not; it requires moist acid conditions; it is very difficult to propagate but
occasionally natural division of the roots takes place

IN the spring of 1788 one of William Curtis's gardeners at his botanic garden
unpacked a consignment of Venus's Fly-traps that miraculously had withstood the
journey from Carolina to London. The plants had been carefully dug so that their roots
were still embedded in a quantity of colonial bog and the gardener observed a number
of knobbly roots, the size and colour of old teeth, in one of the balls of wet soil. He had
the wit to plant them in pots, and force them gently in a tan bed. A few months later
grasslike leaves emerged and two plants produced flowers. The larger and better one
was the subject we see in this excellent plate. It seemed to everyone in the garden as
though it might be an Orchid. Expert opinions were asked for. Sir James Smith,
though much occupied with founding the Linnean Society that same year, declared the
plant was indeed an Orchid. Sir Joseph Banks's Swedish librarian agreed. We may
imagine the gleeful hand-rubbing at the Lambeth Marsh Botanic Garden. In fact it was
a species of Calopogon that had been introduced to the Low Countries as early as 1740
and to England in 1771, but it was not in general cultivation until after this quite
fortuitous introduction in 1788. Doubtless the peculiar circumstances of its arrival
contributed to its popularity. A less observant and imaginative gardener might
reasonably have missed or failed to do anything about the odd little knobs in the soil.
At first it was identified as the West Indian Orchid named by Linnaeus *Limodorum
tuberosum*, and at that stage in the history of botany it was not an unreasonable mistake.
Not much was known about Orchids, certainly not that they comprised the second
largest order of plants in the world and were of such extensive variety. A Brandenburger
botanist, Christian Sprengler, was working at that time on the fertilization of flowers
and published a very accurate account in 1793. This with Charles Darwin's
contribution, *The Various Contrivances by which Orchids are Fertilized by Insects* of 1862,
made correct classification much easier. The 'Limodorum' became a Calopogon with
only three other species in the genus, all of them originally native to bogs and wet
meadows in North America.

Plate 100

Calopogon pulchellus

Fuchsia magellanica Lam. var. *Macrostema* (Ruiz & Pav.) Munz

FUCHSIA

FAMILY: Onagraceae

SYNONYM: *Fuchsia coccinea* Curtis, sensu *Bot. Mag.*, non Aiton

DISTRIBUTION: Chile and Argentina, naturalized elsewhere

CULTIVATION: some races hardy others less so; a tolerant and adaptable shrub, it requires a sunny position but some protection in winter; propagated by cuttings

FRENCH collectors had the distinction of bringing the first two species of *Fuchsia* from Central and South America to Europe, and when this plate was engraved the editor of the *Botanical Magazine* reasonably but mistakenly believed it was one that had been introduced in 1714 and named it *F. coccinea*. It was, in fact, a third species, later named *F. magellanica* as it came from the south of South America, though it is uncertain how it slipped into cultivation. Allegedly it did so about the year 1788 under peculiar circumstances. By then James Lee and his partner Kennedy were leading London nurserymen and the two available species of *Fuchsia* being very fashionable they had stocks of both. Then, by chance, Lee heard of a specimen flowering in the window of a poor woman at Wapping that surpassed the others in beauty. He went there immediately, lost his heart to the Fuchsia, and determined to possess it. But the woman, though poor, was as shrewd as the Scot. Her sailor husband had brought home the plant and she refused to be browbeaten into parting with it. Finally Lee gave her eight guineas down and the promise of the first two pipings that he raised. It was a high price but a good investment. He sliced the plant to bits, potted the pipings and plunged them in a tan bed to start them off in comfortable warmth. By the following flowering season he had 300 plants, two for the grass widow at Wapping, the rest for sale at a guinea apiece. Rumour had it Lee fabricated this story to account for the fact that he had rifled a piping or two of a new species at Kew. His friends suggested he had been sent the original by a professional collector. Whatever the truth of the matter, *F. coccinea* and *F. magellanica* became recognized as separate species and the latter became the hardy parent of scores of hybrids. In 1848 a French expert listed 520 species and cultivars. In the 1880s there were 1,500. One French nursery alone, Lemoine of Nancy, sent out 400 cultivars between 1850 and 1914. Now there are less, and most new hybrids are raised in California, but there are still sufficient to excite Fuchsia fanciers to form a cultus of their own.

Plate 101

Fuchsia magellanica

Hydrangea macrophylla (Thunb.) Ser.

GARDEN HYDRANGEA

FAMILY: Hydrangeaceae
SYNONYM: *Hydrangea hortensis* Smith
DISTRIBUTION: Japan
CULTIVATION: hardy shrub; it requires well-drained soil, a sunny position, and some protection in winter; propagated by cuttings

A LEADING authority on Hydrangeas has declared: '*Variation within the genus is not great.*' Doubtless this is scrupulously correct but to the amateur observer there appears to be colossal variation. For example, one species is grown for the beauty of its ferrous, felted foliage; another because its leaves are shaped like Oak leaves; another is a vigorous climber; and, of those grown chiefly for their flowers, there are the P.G.s with blossoms like a Lilac; Lacecaps with a flat-topped inflorescence; and, a form of this, the bun-shaped Garden Hydrangea that is figured here and was introduced by Sir Joseph Banks in 1789 from China. The plant raised a great furore because the first dried plants and living specimens were oriental cultivars that appeared to consist of sterile blossoms, and, lacking the normal sexual parts, they defied classification. Nevertheless an attempt had to be made to file the enigma in a botanic pigeonhole. Eventually it was decided that the Garden Hydrangea did have small but complete fertile flowers, and that the beautiful blossoms with between three and five 'petals' were actually groups of sepals. The flames of scholarly controversy died low, but they had licked long and far afield over the botanic naming of the plant. The English name of Hydrangea was finally adopted for the genus. But there was no lack of other suggestions. Of those who collected specimens, Kaempfer the German said it was an Elder, Thunberg the Swede said it was a Viburnum, Loureiro the Portuguese said it was a Primula, and Pierre Poivre the Frenchman was happy to use the name bestowed by his fellow countryman Philibert Commerson, naturalist on the French circumnavigation who took with him a young female dressed as a boy and whose sex was discovered in an unseemly scuffle on a South Sea island. Also on the expedition was a Prince of Nassau and it was for his daughter Hortense that Commerson named the plant Hortensia, a name that continues in French, Italian, and German to this day. An alternative story is not without interest: that the naturalist's female companion, in great chagrin at being discovered, changed her name to Hortense, went home to Paris, married a clockmaker, and it was she who was honoured by Commerson's naming.

Plate 102

Hydrangea macrophylla

Campanula mollis L.

SOFT BELL-FLOWER

FAMILY: Campanulaceae
DISTRIBUTION: North Africa, south and south-east Spain
CULTIVATION: not quite hardy perennial; suitable for a cool greenhouse, it prefers a sunny position and a well-drained, calcium-rich potting mixture; propagated by seed or by root division

ALPINE Campanulas are easy to propagate, undemanding, and, given protection in cold areas, will bloom luxuriantly in July and still put out unseasonable flowers during every month of the year. *C. isophylla* is a hairy species that has been a favourite window plant for more than two centuries. It is also magnificent in a hanging basket. Quite recently the Dutch, who are deft at such things, have tamed the non-hairy *C. fragilis*, grow them in pots, a white form, and one of Cambridge blue trained up stakes, and sell them as 'bride and groom'.[1] Alpine Campanulas are legion and identifying the species is necessarily the work of an expert. There is not much agreement about the *C. mollis* figured here. The *Botanical Magazine* informs us it was introduced in 1788 from Syria, Sicily, and Spain, which is agreeably sibilant and sounds like an elocution exercise for Eliza Doolittle, but factually is somewhat doubtful. We are informed by gardening dictionaries that *C. mollis* is a synonym of *C. lanata* and of *C. velutina*. This is unlikely because the last two come from different parts of the Mediterranean region and do not exactly correspond. To the collector the sad thing is that *C. mollis* appears to have almost disappeared both from seed-lists and from Spain. It is only to be hoped that, like other rare Alpine species, it does still thrive in some secret place. *C. fragilis*, in the wild, is rare because it has a very restricted distribution. But at its headquarters, which shall remain unpublished, it is as prolific as rice in China. The conditions that suit them best are a firm anchorage, a little humus in the crevice to feed on, baking summers, and drenching rains in autumn. They also have to be knocked about by stiff breezes because in pendant species the seed capsule only shoots out its seeds from the base and thus needs a thorough shaking. Like cage birds and butterflies pinned to cork, Alpine Campanulas in captivity cannot compare with those growing in the wild. These hang in festoons from limestone cliffs, their flowers chiefly a watchet blue but with occasional variations from a milky white through to a grey-violet, and dot the stone like mosaic work or, if there are scores of plants, almost cover it in rivers of bright colour.

---

[1] *C. fragilis* is frequently misnamed *C. isophylla* by the trade, either through ignorance or, more likely, deliberately because the latter is a more familiar name to the market.

Plate 103

Campanula mollis

Blakea trinerva L.

JAMAICAN ROSE

FAMILY: Melastomataceae
DISTRIBUTION: Jamaica
CULTIVATION: non-hardy, scandent shrub or epiphyte; it requires a heated greenhouse, and it is better to train it up a trellis although it is able to support itself if pruned; propagated by seed or by cuttings

BLAKEAS belong to a family of plants that have little or no economic or medicinal use and, like the equally useless, debonair wasters who once sponged on a glittering high society, they have a grace and a charm all of their own. The Melastomataceae include Medinillas, Miconias, Bertolinas, Sonerilas, Centradinias, Osbeckias, and Tibouchinas that stud the tropical and subtropical rain forests and marshes right round the globe in jewels of colour, and yield nothing to man save a few rather fugitive dyes but a great aesthetic pleasure. They are characterized by the marking of their simple leaves, lacking true mid-ribs and with veins that run longitudinally to meet at the leaf point. The Blakea figured here has its specific name because of the three distinct veins in its evergreen leaves. Members of the family are also characterized by the regularity of their flowers, there being twice as many stamens as there are petals. The Blakeas are unusual in that they have six petals and twelve stamens. The great majority only have four or five petals.

The plate shows a detail of what a very large plant can be. Though its leaves are glossy above and below, the stems are covered with auburn hair and the flower stems are noticeably longer than the leaf stems. As the plant ages the main stem branches and continues to do so into a huge system of ramification, and the branches produce roots like Old Man's Beard. This tells us it is not, as it is usually described, a shrub but a climber that needs support and in nature sprawls over a host. In other words, it is a flopper that grows to a great height if its feet are in water and its head, or chief growing point, is struggling upwards towards the sun. In Jamaica, the country of its provenance, it thrives in cool, humid, and shady situations, and, the larger it becomes, the more rosy flowers it displays.

William Aiton, the King's gardener, received a plant of the species from the West Indies in 1789 and grew it with other Jamaican plants. It was named for Martin Blake, a settler in Antigua who was a naturalist and a patron of collectors in the West Indies. He could scarcely have been given a more glorious memorial. A contemporary described the splendour of the plant: *'This vegetable is certainly one of the most beautiful productions of America.'*

Plate 104

Blakea trinerva

Chrysanthemum vestitum-indicum group

AUTUMN-FLOWERING CHRYSANTHEMUM

FAMILY: Compositae
DISTRIBUTION: Japan, China, and Indonesia
CULTIVATION: perennial of obscure origin; cultivars related to the species should be
raised and propagated according to the horticultural section into which they fall

THE appearance of the Chrysanthemum, like the frontiers of Europe, has altered
with the passage of time. Men have altered both. In the Far East the plant has been
cultivated for more than 2,500 years, the Chinese esteeming it though not quite so
much as the Japanese. About the time Charlemagne was crowned in the West the
Mikado took the flower as his personal emblem, decreed that no commoner might grow
it, and instituted the Order of the Chrysanthemum. It even became the national flag
and makes the point that all the song lyrics, poems, newspaper articles, and travelogues
that refer to 'The Land of the Rising Sun' ought, properly, to be entitled 'The Land of
the Chrysanthemum with Sixteen Petals'. Within a hundred years the Japanese were
holding Chrysanthemum shows. The first to be held in the West was in Norwich in
1843 almost a thousand years later. The name Chrysanthemum means 'golden flower'
but Oriental gardeners were soon crossing and re-crossing species and stunting plants
to produce larger blooms. Before 1700 the Dutch naturalist Rumpf in Amboina
described a red variety, possibly the one here figured, and others of white and ash-
green, and one with petals that drooped in the forenoon and evening but stood erect at
midday and was called by the natives 'The Drunken Woman'. He described
entertainments where the guests measured their importance and their host's affection
by the size of the Chrysanthemum on the table. Its petals were also eaten either lightly
fried or raw as a spicy flavour to salading. Considering its widespread culture in the
Orient and the number of botanical explorers who sent plants from the East the
Chrysanthemum was slow in being established in the West. There were introductions
to Holland in 1688 and to England in 1764 but both failed. Then a Marseilles shipper
received three varieties in 1789: one purple, one violet, one white. Only the purple
survived and was sent in 1790 to the Jardin Royal[1] in Paris. By the end of the 18th
century about eight varieties had been established in France and in other countries.
They were themselves garden cultivars as a wild Chrysanthemum should look like a
daisy with disk florets and ray florets. Western hybridists got to work and there is
hardly any room to doubt that *C. vestitum-indicum* is related to all the massive autumn-
flowering Chrysanthemums of today: the pets of show exhibitors and standfast of the
cut-flower trade.

[1] Only royal until 25 September 1792 when it became known as Muséum d'histoire naturelle.

Plate 105

Chrysanthemum vestitum-indicum

Sparmannia africana L.fil.

AFRICAN HEMP

FAMILY: Tiliaceae
DISTRIBUTION: South Africa
CULTIVATION: non-hardy shrub or tree; suitable for a cool greenhouse or it can be
cultivated as a house-plant; propagated by cuttings or by seed

AFRICAN Hemp is a tall and evergreen winter-flowering pot plant in the northern
hemisphere that is tough enough to stand a certain amount of cold and even neglect. In
South Africa it grows to 16 metres (20 feet) and more. In a greenhouse and stopped at
3 metres (8 feet) it will make a wrist-sized mainbranch and many branchlets. The
leaves, stems, even the calyx of four sepals are covered densely with hair that to the
touch is rougher than velvet but of the same texture. The petals are papery and white
and fold back to reveal a mass of sensitive flower parts that resemble a gold cushion
stuck with chocolate and violet pins. The style and stigma are longer than the pins and
the colour of Gooseberry. A curious feature of the blossom is that it flowers
downwards, rather than upwards, as a Foxglove does. The top flowers open first. The
foliage is even odder. The leaf edges are jagged but their shape is not consistent. Those
closest to the flowers are heart-shaped but, here and there on the same shrub, are leaves
as palmate as those of a Maple. Presumably the foliage is variable. The genus is named,
and misspelt, for one of Linnaeus's heroic disciples, Anders Sparrman. At the age of
17 he served his apprenticeship as surgeon and plant-hunter in a two-year journey to
China in 1765. He returned with a rich haul of plants, was highly praised, and sent off
to South Africa. There he had an unlooked-for opportunity for adventure. Captain
Cook came ashore at the Cape on his way out on the second circumnavigation. His
naturalists were principally zoologists. Cook invited Sparrman to join the expedition as
botanist. Off he went. A glance at a map of that voyage shows how for two years they
meandered round the South Atlantic and the Great South Sea. Eventually Sparrman
found himself back at the Cape of Good Hope. He botanised there for eight months
before returning home, and was to see a lot more of Africa before he settled into a
quieter, donnish life in Stockholm.

Plate 106

Sparmannia africana

Pterospermum acerifolium Willd.

MAPLE-LEAVED PTEROSPERMUM

FAMILY: Sterculiaceae
DISTRIBUTION: continental South and South-east Asia
CULTIVATION: non-hardy tree; requires a warm greenhouse and a great deal of space before it flowers; propagated by seed or by cuttings

ALTHOUGH nothing merely political, even bloody revolutions, could deflect the single-mindedness of collectors and gardeners in the early 1790s, North America and much of Europe were in too much of a state of ferment for the calm enjoyment of botany and horticulture. And in England it happened that great patrons and the great gardeners with green fingers were becoming thinner on the ground. Sir Joseph Banks still had his grip on botanical affairs and shook them from time to time, as a terrier does a rat, to prove his power; but Solander was no longer at his shoulder. Sir James Smith nursed his young Linnean Society and William Aiton, who had spent forty years managing Kew and accommodating Banks, was feeling his age. Amongst the nurserymen Loddiges and Graefer were doing well, and Lee and Kennedy tending to live on their fat because they, too, were feeling old. Nevertheless it was they who had the fortune to introduce *Pterospermum acerifolium* into cultivation as a stove plant. An East Indian agent sent seeds to their nursery in 1796 and there they were germinated and grown as foliage shrubs for stoves. In their tropical homeland Pterospermums made great trees with fragrant white flowers but they did not bloom under glass and Lee died in 1795, never knowing that such a thing was possible. Then, by accident or because of a more intuitive understanding of the plant's needs, twelve years after its introduction a specimen did bloom in the collection of a rival firm, Whitley and Brames. Sydenham Edwards at once went round to immortalize it with his pencil. The result is a most interesting design, the flower being superimposed on one large leaf; the two almost filling the whole page. Long before its introduction into cultivation the Pterospermum had been known to botanists by description, drawings, and dried specimens. It had gone through the mincing machine of nomenclature and collected quite a few names before *P. acerifolium* was agreed upon. The leaf in the plate is less lobed than that of a field Maple as the specific name suggests. Nevertheless it is very fine; leathery and with an uneven number of veins, its underside covered with a smooth mass of fair hairs that extend all over the back of the stems and bough and trunk. The calyx is also leathery and sheaths the petals of the flowers. It makes a most decorative shrub.

Plate 107

Pterospermum acerifolium

PURPLE MAGNOLIA

FAMILY: Magnoliaceae
SYNONYMS: *Magnolia purpurea* Curt., *M. discolor* Vent.
DISTRIBUTION: native in East China, naturalized in Japan
CULTIVATION: hardy deciduous shrub or small tree; the flowers are frequently
damaged by late frosts, and it should therefore be planted in a somewhat shaded
position; propagated by seed, layering, or grafting

IN countries where every house has its garden and it has become the custom to grow
shrubs and bulbs rather than a flower or vegetable garden, species of this grand genus
are becoming almost too ubiquitous. Each one deserves and requires to be enjoyed
individually and if every little garden has one it becomes impossible. Therefore the
splendid evergreen North American species that are chiefly used to clothe large houses,
or the rare and exquisite Asian species, are to be preferred to the popular species and
hybrids that in affluent society have swept across continents and become as common as
Goosegrass. The graceful species figured here was introduced from China in 1790 by
the 3rd Duke of Portland during a rare interval when he was resting from statecraft
because he was Home Secretary for a long period and twice Prime Minister. Magnolias
were cultivated by the Japanese but native to China and therefore there must always be
some doubt about the provenance of a plant sent to the West so long ago. It was
immediately hailed by horticulturalists for its qualities which are quiet rather than
loud, and by botanists who rejoice over its primitive features and rate it as a fossil with
the Maidenhair Tree. Structurally it is also interesting, particularly the oblong
conglomeration of carpels that open on one side and from which seeds dangle from
threads. It makes a large deciduous bush with many glass-green leaves that have a
slight down above and on the veins below. The flowers are sometimes chalice-shaped,
less often like upturned bells; but mostly they are looser in shape so that they resemble
untidy Fosteriana Tulips. The inside of the flower is white, the outside purple marked
with deeper streaks, and the sepals are a light green. It is a very beautiful plant indeed,
that has gone through about half a dozen ceremonious namings beginning with *M.*
purpurea and ending as *M. liliflora*. It was almost as certain as the law of gravity that the
hybridists should be struck by that unique wine-purple colour and somehow introduce
it into a more garish strain. But there is a story, which romantics prefer, that in 1797,
in the garden of a French gentleman named M. Soulange-Bodin quite close to Paris,
two Chinese Magnolias enjoyed a clandestine affair. They were *M. liliflora* and *M.*
denudata, and from that springtime liaison their love-child was the waxy, shapely, and
very ubiquitous *M. ✕. soulangiana*.

Plate 108

Magnolia liliflora

Hardenbergia violacea (Schneev.) Stearn

PURPLE GLYCINE

FAMILY: Leguminosae
SYNONYMS: *Glycine virens* Solander, G. *bimaculata* Curtis, *Kennedya monophylla* Vent.
DISTRIBUTION: Australia and Tasmania
CULTIVATION: non-hardy, evergreen, straggling shrub; requires a light, well-ventilated position in a cool greenhouse; propagated by seed or by cuttings

THE wings and heel of the flowers indicate that this plant belongs to the family of Peas. The small blooms are prettily coloured and have a scent that is slightly fugitive save in full sunlight, and their arrangement in upstanding racemes is in direct contrast to the simple, spear-shaped leaves that almost invariably hang downwards, and is an example of classic proportion in nature. The writer of the original letterpress that accompanied this plate regretted its small size and '*the imperfection of the colouring art*'. He need not have apologised. It is an excellently arranged and coloured deisgn of a twiner without its support. *H. violacea* is one of those plants with a leading stem that spirals in an arc until it meets something to embrace and use as an anchor. For want of anything else it will even twine about another of its own leading stems and the two consolidate to make a thick rope of some rigidity. This is quite often noticed in Wistarias and therefore it is not surprising to learn that the plant was at first considered a member of the same genus, *Glycine*. In fact it is one of two species of a genus peculiar to Australia and Tasmania, or, as they were called at that time, New Holland and Van Diemen's Land. In the wild the species flops over low bushes, twining itself about them, and after its introduction into cultivation in 1790 it was used as a decorative evergreen twiner to clothe the columns and walls of a cool house, or grown in pots on supports to make pyramids or globes of colour. Its late arrival from the Antipodes has yet to be satisfactorily explained. It was known to Dr Solander who first named it, and there was always a brisk traffic in 'Botany Bay' seeds, yet the two *Hardenbergia* species were late to arrive. Possibly Dr Solander's increasing lassitude might have accounted for it. His lack of vigour was so pronounced that Linnaeus found it necessary to write to a friend in London asking him to urge Solander to write to his mother '*who has not received a word from her beloved son for several years*'. Indeed this was true, and, after his death, several of his mother's letters to Solander were found unopened. A man of such constitutional apathy was unlikely to have any energy for organizing the introduction of exotics. Indeed it is remarkable that he ever managed to work over the plants he and Banks found on their voyage round the world, and equally remarkable to the layman that so sluggish a man should actually die of apoplexy which he managed to do in 1782, eight years before this species was introduced.

Plate 109

Hardenbergia violacea

Rhinacanthus nastulus (L.) O. Kuntze.

RINGWORM ROOT

FAMILY: Acanthaceae
SYNONYMS: *Justicia nastula* L., *Rhinacanthus communis* Nees
DISTRIBUTION: South and South-east Asia and Republic of Malagasy
CULTIVATION: non-hardy shrub; requires a warm greenhouse; propagated by seed or by cuttings

RINGWORM Root was introduced in 1790 by yet another adventurous Scot of humble birth named William Roxburgh. He read medicine at Edinburgh and as a green boy of 15 became Surgeon's Mate on an East India Company ship trading between the subcontinent and Britain. In 1776 he was based ashore as assistant to the Company's Surgeon at Madras. India was by no means the huge red blob on the map she was to become. The largest Company territories were in Bengal, and the strip of northern Circas recently taken from the French. The Madras territory was small and hemmed in by Dutch and French possessions and by lands held by the Mogul. In Roxburgh's lifetime the map was to alter with extraordinary rapidity. In 1781 he began to specialise in botany and so proved his worth that the Company appointed him botanist of the Coast of Coromandel when that territory was seized from the Mogul. He made large collections of plants, hired native artists to draw and paint living specimens, and himself drew dissections of floral parts. Much of his work was eaten by ants or flooded in monsoons but he had the wisdom to send a parcel of the paintings to Sir Joseph Banks in England. The action fixed his destiny: Banks at once arranged for 300 plates to be made and published. Pressure was brought so that Roxburgh duly became Superintendent of the Calcutta Botanic Garden. An evergreen Indian vine was named for him *Roxburghia* because it symbolized his steady climb to the top of his profession. He amassed an enormous collection of plants and drawings and notes for a *Flora Indica* that is still useful. But, unlike many other collectors, he made the time to enjoy himself in Calcutta society, marrying three wives and begetting four sons and four daughters. As was common amongst Company employees, his health broke down and he retired, taking an extensive botanical tour via the Cape and the island of St. Helena before he reached Scotland and died. Roxburgh was responsible for many Indian plants being brought into cultivation in the West. If they were useful as well as beautiful he was particularly pleased. He considered the Ringworm Root a fine shrub and, used in conjunction with pepper and lime juice, as a sovereign control for ringworm. He also observed: *'Milk boiled on the roots is reckoned, by the Indian physicians aphrodisiacal.'* He did not say the claim was frivolous, but added the plain comment: *'No medicines are more sought after by the natives.'*

Plate 110

Rhinacanthus nastulus

Billardiera scandens Smith

APPLE-BERRY

FAMILY: Pittosporaceae
DISTRIBUTION: Tasmania, eastern and southern Australia
CULTIVATION: non-hardy, somewhat straggling climber; suitable for a cool
greenhouse, it requires lime-free, sandy soil; propagated by seed or by cuttings

CAPTAIN Cook, Joseph Banks, and Dr Solander had been critical of the soil and freshwater supplies but otherwise only had the happiest memories of Botany Bay where they made landfall in April 1770, chased off a few natives, netted quantities of fish and found shellfish in the champagne bubbling sea, saw a multitude of plants and strange beasts and so many exotic birds that a huge parrot pie was baked in the galley of the *Endeavour*. Eleven years afterwards the British withdrew from the American colonies and found themselves obliged to find an alternative penal settlement. Banks proposed New Holland. It was remote and there was plenty of room for convicts. Thus Botany Bay, once idyllic and untouched by European civilization, was brutalized by gaolbirds and their keepers and became the subject of many haunting 19th century ballads.

The botanical exploration first begun there was continued along the littoral and sometimes into the interior. In 1790, through the agency of Banks, the plant figured here was introduced to Europe and written up by Sir James Smith in his list of New Holland plants. He named it for the former royal Director-General of royal establishments and gardens in Paris, Jacques-Julien Houton de la Billardière, who after the Revolution busied himself with travel and specialized in the plants of Syria and New Holland. Sir James also noted a curious fact that hitherto had been overloooked. The *Billardiera* was '*almost the only eatable fruit that grows spontaneously in this country, so famous for stealing the eye of the botanist*'. In Australia it is said to taste of roasted apples, but in cultivation its flavour is insipid. The plate shows a fruit not quite fully mature. Botanically this is a berry, not such an obvious one as a Mulberry but more like a Tomato or Grape or Cucumber.

In nature the plant is a climber, half twiner, half flopper, that sprawls over surrounding shrubs. Grown as an evergreen in a protected part of a garden it tends to turn itself into a low bush with tortuous, hairy branches. From the ends of the branches hang the bell-shaped, cream-violet flowers. Another species, *B. longiflora*, is altogether tougher and has two varieties, one with white berries, and the other with red.

Plate 111

Billardiera scandens

Cipura paludosa Aublet

FAMILY: Iridaceae
SYNONYM: *Marica paludosa* (Aublet) Willd.
DISTRIBUTION: Tropical South America and West Indies
CULTIVATION: non-hardy bulb; requires a warm greenhouse, it should be kept
somewhat dry in winter; propagated by bulb offsets or by seed

THERE are four species of *Cipura* but, beyond the ranks of Iris specialists, it is improbable that any but the plant figured here is being cultivated. It is a native of South America being discovered in Guyanan foothill grasslands by a French botanist, M. Aublet. He described and named the plant and noted that there is a blue variety. In 1792 it was introduced into cultivation in Europe by Alexander Anderson, Superintendent of the British Government Botanic Garden at St. Vincent in the Windward Isles, who, though it hardly requires saying, owed his post to Sir Joseph Banks and was his regular correspondent. Anderson sent a number of genera to Europe and the inclusion of *C. paludosa* showed he had a stylish sense of what makes a handsome plant. We are not shown the swollen tuber that is covered with a netting of membrane, but the foliage is bold and the flower, in proportion, very dainty. The flower parts are so petal-like they are difficult to distinguish, but they are regular and arranged with exactitude in threes. There are three sepals, three petals, three stamens, even a three-cleft style.

The specific name *paludosa* infers that in nature the plant is a denizen of fens and we rather naturally associate such a habitat with tacky mud and what the Old Testament descriptively terms slimepits. The mistake is seen when fenland is reclaimed. It shrinks perceptibly into a fibrous loam or into fine silt, either of which consists of mineral and organic particles with impure air and water in the spaces between. Therefore a gardener can meet the soil requirements of a fen plant without any difficulty, but the plant never loses one characteristic, an inclination to flower later in the year than plants growing in dry soil. This is because its habitat is annually swamped, and growth cannot begin until the flood recedes and the ground gradually dries out. Then, like all other plants, it absorbs minerals and moisture from the soil and carbon dioxide from the air and the energy of the sun transforms this into tissue that makes leaf and stem and flower.

Because it is late to bloom, and in order to ensure fertilization after what might be called the height of the pollinating season, the *Cipura* is an hermaphrodite with the means to reproduce itself should that be necessary.

Plate 112

Cipura paludosa

Cobaea scandens Cav.

CLIMBING COBAEA, CUP-AND-SAUCER PLANT

FAMILY: Polemoniaceae
DISTRIBUTION: Mexico, naturalized elsewhere
CULTIVATION: in a heated greenhouse it is a woody, perennial climber but it is easily cultivated out of doors as a summer annual; propagated by seed or by cuttings

ABOUT 1650 a scholarly Jesuit, Father Cobo, completed more than forty years' missionary work in the Spanish American Empire and, simultaneously, the last volume of ten on the natural history of the New World. One hundred and fifty years later his work was still extant but unpublished, but the neglected naturalist's name lived on in a genus *Cobaea* of eighteen fascinating and attractive species of climbing shrubs. One species in particular invites the attention of gardeners because it can be grown as a perennial in a greenhouse, or out of doors as an annual, and is singularly free of all plant diseases. The uncoloured leaf in the background of the figure is but one of a number of alternate pinnate leaves that end in branched tendrils. The tendrils are leaf-structures, like those of a Sweet Pea, and are extremely sensitive, nodding or bobbing up and down of their own volition searching for a support. The instant contact is made the hook anchors the tendril while it clasps the support and forms a coil. This is one of the most rapid of all climbers reaching 8 metres (25 feet) in a season and its liveliness and vigour are observable to the human eye. Because the tube of petals sits so neatly in the sepals it is sometimes known as the Cup-and-Saucer Plant, but it has other far more noticeable features. It seems to be constantly on the move. The closed bud stands vertically on its red stem but bends as soon as it begins to open and goes through 180° before it is fully open. The bell-shaped flowers have long stamens and styles that also keep moving, and the striped tube actually changes colour and its smell in the course of time for the specific purpose of ensuring pollination. When the flower is basically green and smells unpleasant it is attracting insects. It then converts to bee-pollination by smelling sweetly of honey and changing its colour to imperial purple. Even then the plant cannot keep still and the stems gyrate when the fruit is formed in shape and colour like a gherkin. Strangely, this restless exotic was late in being established in European gardens. Different dates for its introduction have been proposed by different authorities, doubtless because some failed, and others were restricted and local. Therefore it seems sensible to record the latest suggested date, 1792,[1] as the most acceptable for the plant's general and successful introduction into cultivation.

[1] From William Aiton's *Hortus Kewensis*, second edition.

Plate 113

Cobaea scandens

Lagunaria patersonii G. Don

NORFOLK ISLAND HIBISCUS

FAMILY: Malvaceae
DISTRIBUTION: Eastern Australia, Norfolk Island, and Lord Howe Island
CULTIVATION: non-hardy evergreen tree; suitable for a large cool greenhouse; propagated by seed or by cuttings

THERE is only one species of this genus and it is found in three places separated by large distances. It was first collected from Norfolk Island, a lonely pimple in the South Pacific. It also grows on Lord Howe Island, an equally isolated pimple not quite 1,100 kilometres (600 miles) to the south-west. And the same species, or a form of it, is found in the tropical part of the Australian state of Queensland, 1,500 kilometres (800 miles) to the north-west of Lord Howe Island.

The Lagunaria is a handsome tree growing to 16 metres (50 feet) in the right habitat but in less bland climates it is not quite hardy and needs the protection of a greenhouse. The evergreen leaves are very handsome, the dotted dark green of the upperside contrasting well with the scaly underside the colour of woodash. Their veins stand out as prominently as those of a choleric old man. It is marvellous that a good foliage tree should have such exquisite flowers. The plant shows they spring from the leaf axils which is a characteristic of many of the most ornamental trees, but the lack of any sort of scale prevents us from realizing each flower is about 7.5 centimetres (3 inches) across. The five curving petals enclose many stamens that are shorter than the style. It is not surprising to learn that the plant belongs to the Mallow family that contains such outstanding garden plants as the Hollyhock, Hibiscus, and Abutilon.

The two names of this tree marry two distinguished but very dissimilar botanists. Andrés de Laguna was a Spanish physician and naturalist appointed as medical attendant to Pope Julius III, very much a Renaissance figure entirely at ease both at courts and in the society of scholars. Lieutenant William Paterson was a contemporary of Carl Peter Thunberg and by nature a loner. He escaped from society by burying himself in the South African veldt botanising with a Dutch soldier amongst the Caffraria and Hottentots. If he made collections of dried plants or drawings and notes none still exist. Then he became conscious that there were too many collectors at the Cape and took himself off on a solitary adventure in the South Seas. In 1792, at the age of 37, and by then a Colonel by purchase, his voyages came to an end. He returned to England laden with seeds. Amongst them were seeds of the *Lagunaria* he had found on Norfolk Island. A specimen grown in a London nursery flowered for the first time nine years later.

Plate 114

Lagunaria patersonii

Cymbidium aloifolium (L.) Sw.

FAMILY: Orchidaceae
SYNONYMS: *Epidendrum aloifolium* L., *E. aloides* Curt.
DISTRIBUTION: Peninsular India and Sri Lanka
CULTIVATION: non-hardy perennial; requires a warm greenhouse, prefers a loose, fibrous potting mixture; propagated by division

THERE are about forty Cymbidiums that originated in Asia or Australia. Probably to most people they are *the* Orchid because they are the flower of the bouquet, spray, and buttonhole, and seem to be the most expensive flower for sale. In view of the fact that a cut flower will last for eight weeks in water and three months if it is growing in a pot, they are not all that expensive. They are the hardiest of exotic orchids, mostly flower in the winter, live comfortably in a greenhouse, and hybridisers have crossed some stunted species and concocted pygmy Cymbidiums that are undemanding house-plants. The colour combinations of cultivars are ambitious. Amongst them are flowers of white touched with raspberry pink; lemon yellow streaked and spotted with blood red; gold marked with crimson; salmon with rose-pink veins and stripes, greenish-white petals and sepals surrounding a lip of peat brown and yellow. For this gaudiness some have paid the sacrifice of a certain amount of fragrance. The species are equally hardy, and more beautifully scented, though they do not have as many nor such large flowers on a single spray. Many have pseudo-bulbs for storing water and other reserves and are essentially tropical plants, but they defy easy identification and orchidists go hammer and tongs at one another about 'correct' names. We have boldly selected one specific name from a variety of possibilities for naming this plate and are confident we shall cause disagreement.

Because the Orchid order has its fertilization so intimately linked with insects both colour and smell must have an appeal to a special pollinating agent. In the case of the *Cymbidium* it must be a fly or a bee because the flower lacks a spur, and only Orchids with spurs are pollinated by butterflies and moths that have a long proboscis. The deed done, and the process of fertilizing completed, each capsule produces between one and a half and one and three-quarter million little seeds. This species was one of the first, if not the first, *Cymbidium* to be introduced into European glasshouses. In 1793 it reached England from India and was coaxed into growth and finally into bloom. It was noted in India that, though it would scramble through other trees, it had one favourite support, and liked to settle on and writhe through the branches of *Strychnos nox-vomica*, the chief source of strychnine.

Plate 115

Cymbidium aloifolium

Gladiolus cuspidatus Jacq.

FAMILY: Iridaceae

DISTRIBUTION: South Africa

CULTIVATION: non-hardy corm; suitable for a cool greenhouse and the pot can be put outside in summer; propagated by corm offsets or by seed

MANY, many species of *Gladiolus* were introduced from South Africa in the late 18th century, and a great many were the subjects of plates in the *Botanical Magazine*. They ranged in height from specimens only a few centimetres high to the Parrot Gladiolus which reached 120 centimetres (4 feet). Some had very few flowers at the tip of the stem, others were borne alongside the stem mostly facing one way. The variation in colour was as large. There were shades of white, green, yellow, purple, pink, and scarlet but no real blue. The flowers were equally diverse in shape; some conventionally funnel-shaped, others starry, others as it were hooded, some open, and there were oddities like the pretty species shown in the plate. Cultivars have since been developed that are triumphs of the hybridizer's skill, though a blue variety has yet to be found, and they have a large following. *Gladiolus* species are less flamboyant, and as they bloom in winter and early spring and require a greenhouse, they are neglected save by a few collectors. Regrettably, to the general gardening public the majority are unavailable. *G. cuspidatus* is a fair example of this vanished race. It grows knee-high and the three or four sword leaves almost reach the height of the flowering stem. The flowers grow from one side of the stem on long stalks. These swell into a wide funnel of segments that are either wavy, as in the plate, or simply loose and flagging. Occasionally the flowers are fragrant, but this is never certain and it cannot be counted among the delightfully scented species from the Cape. *G. cuspidatus* was taken to England in 1795 by Francis Masson when he returned from his second tour of duty at the Cape. In this volume only a very small number of his fine introductions are shown. He served Kew well, making many botanical explorations all for £100 a year for himself and £200 for expenses. He suffered many hardships, on one occasion being hunted by a chain-gang of desperate convicts at the Cape, on another being taken a prisoner of war by the French, on another being captured by privateers, and, finally, in the bad winter of 1805, he froze to death in Canada.

Plate 116

Gladiolus cuspidatus

Stapelia verrucosa Masson var. *Robusta* N.E. Br.

WARTY CARRION FLOWER

FAMILY: Asclepiadaceae
DISTRIBUTION: South Africa: Cape Province
CULTIVATION: non-hardy perennial; it likes full light and can be kept on a windowsill or
close to the glass of a heated greenhouse, it must be kept relatively dry, especially in
winter; propagated by cuttings

SUCCULENTS are either gazing stocks or they are choice objects to the collector who
seeks them out, grows them, invests in rarities, prizes natural hybrids but despises
man-made cultivars, and probably joins local societies of like-minded people. That
they have a totally different appeal from other more orthodox plants is made evident by
remarks passed by visitors to the succulent house of a botanic garden. Hardly any other
innocent eavesdropping can give such a range of entertainment. To lovers of the quaint
and curious Carrion Flowers are fascinating plants being both weird in appearance and
perfectly constructed to withstand the semi-arid conditions of their provenance. The
stems of the Warty Carrion Flower in the plate are a Chartreuse colour when plumped
out with reserves of water, and this green tissue does the work done by leaves in other
plants; that is, build up organic substances from inorganic sources. In fact, the plant
does have leaves but they are minute degenerate structures that shrivel and fall off and
serve no purpose. Utility is everything to the Carrion Flower. It is constructed to make
the most of sudden supplies of water in either infrequent rainstorms or heavy dew,
otherwise to cut down evaporation. The warts on stems and flowers help by reflecting
the rays of the sun. The horny skin of older plants is a bad conductor of heat. And
mathematically it presents the minimum surface area for the sun to play on as the
flower base and the corona are cupola-shaped and even the star petals curve back in an
arc. All species attract pollinating flies by the yellow or livid colouring of their starfish-
like flowers and by giving off a stench of rotting flesh or fish. Not unexpectedly they
are frequently visited by Blow-flies. Carrion Flowers have two other intriguing
features. One is that they sometimes go into a dormant state before the fruit is fully
developed, but start off again as soon as growth recommences. The second is that no
sooner is the seed ripe and dispersed than it germinates with remarkable acceleration.
Within twenty-four hours all is completed. In the case of ordinary garden Parsley the
gardener must wait about thirteen weeks. Introduced in 1795 from the Cape at the
same time as the Dewy species the Warty Carrion Flower enjoyed only a *succès d'estime*
among the botanical gentlemen of Europe.

Plate 117

Stapelia verrucosa

Gentiana decumbens L.

FAMILY: Gentianaceae
SYNONYM: *Gentiana adscendens* Pall.
DISTRIBUTION: Himalaya region, Mongolia, and Siberia
CULTIVATION: hardy perennial; it is a tolerant and adaptable plant that thrives in moist, clay soil and prefers a sunny position; propagated by seed or by careful division of the root

GENTIANS are named after a King of Illyricum who was credited with the discovery of their medicinal value. He was equally famous in history as the intrepid defier of the might of Republican Rome by imprisoning her ambassadors. He paid for it by being paraded with all his family as the prisoners of Rome in a spectacular triumph. It seems that all species of the genus do contain a bitter principle that acts as a tonic. Generally this is too sharp to be palatable without adding a flavour such as orange peel, but *G. decumbens*, a Siberian species, is fortunate in that its bitter principle is also aromatic, and at the time of its introduction to Europe it was noted that the plant was regularly used as a tonic, an appetizer, and a digestive by the inhabitants of Siberia. Agents of the Hanoverian gardener Conrad Loddiges sent him plants or, more likely, seeds in 1799. It was the year of the death of his friend William Curtis, the last in the Golden Century of Botany. By then Loddiges had established himself as a supplier of rare plants. In 1777 he had issued an impressive *Catalogue of Plants and Seeds* in English and in German. In 1817 he was to publish an ambitious monthly catalogue with engraved plates and letterpress entitled *The Botanical Cabinet*. His nurseries grew to fill 6.1 hectares (15 acres) and it was there that he grew and afterwards distributed this Siberian Gentian. The plant we see in the plate was grown by him as he sent a pair to Dr John Sims, the new editor of the *Botanical Magazine*. Dr Sims noted they differed and classed them as (*var.* α) which is shown in this plate and which, because of its upright stems and flowers, was aptly given the specific name *adscendens*. Evidently the second (*var.* β) was weaker, lay flat, and was named *decumbens*. In fact the stalks of the species are decumbent before they are ascendant, but it seems eggs in moonshine to name what ends as a manifestly upright plant *decumbens*. The basal leaf, shown apart, is long and handsome, the stem leaves are smaller and curly and resemble those of a Carnation. The calyx is curious in that it has a split down one side like some kinds of skirt. The deep blue colour is characteristic of the European and Asian Gentians that have blue or yellow or soft lilac shades. New Zealand Gentians are white. Those from South America are brighter and include vermilion.

Plate 118

Gentiana decumbens

Zenobia pulverulenta (Willd.) Pollard

FAMILY: Ericaceae
SYNONYMS: *Andromeda pulverulenta* Willd., *A. dealbata* Lindl.
DISTRIBUTION: U.S.A from North Carolina to Florida
CULTIVATION: hardy shrub; requires well-drained but moist, lime-free soil and some shade; propagated by seed or by offsets

JOHN Bartram, the self-taught botanist of Philadelphia, saw this lovely North American shrub and described it. Most probably he also sent seeds to his patrons in England but, if so, the introduction was a failure. It remained for John Fraser, the draper turned collector, and his son John to make a successful introduction in 1800. The detail in the plate was actually drawn at the Frasers' house in London. The plant makes a sturdy bush between 1.4 and 2 metres high (4 and 6 feet) and in June and July it produces from the ends of the previous year's shoots a raceme of flowers that are shaped like Lilies of the Valley and are clustered together in groups of hanging bells. The sepals are very slightly wrinkled and the colour of freshwater weeds. They cup the white corollas that turn back at the edge into five lobes and contain ten stamens with brown anthers. The flowers are fragrant with a sweet, not overpowering trace of the scent of aniseed. The foliage commands equal attention.

Probably *Zenobia* is a genus of only one species and the plant figured is a form known as *pulverulenta* because, from a distance, it looks dusty. This is caused by the exceedingly fine light hairs that cover the foliage and shoots. The veined underside of the leaves is the colour of a Carlesbad Plum and has the same bloom that can be rubbed off with a thumb; the upperside is a leaden blue green. There is another form that lacks this bloom, and another with leaves of a slightly different shape, but neither quite match the *pulverulenta*. Formerly plants were grown in pots and forced for spring shows, but they are hardy and can also be grown outside in lime-free gardens. Being partially evergreen they have an advantage over purely deciduous flowering shrubs, and, planted against the right background, their beauty is dramatic. But fashion is as potent amongst nurserymen as amongst couturiers, and at the time of writing, this American plant commands far less attention than it truly deserves.

At first the plant was classed with the *Andromeda* genus. Then David Don, Librarian of the Linnean Society, worked it over and decided it should stand as a genus on its own. He chose a not inappropriate name for so distinguished a shrub: Zenobia, Queen of Palmyra, sprung from the Ptolemies of Egypt, Regent of the Eastern Roman Empire, a resourceful sovereign, learned, warlike, proud, and beautiful.

Plate 119

Zenobia pulverulenta

Epacris purpurescens R. Br.

RIGID EPACRIS

FAMILY: Epacridaceae
SYNONYM: *Epacris pungens* Cav.
DISTRIBUTION: Australia: New South Wales
CULTIVATION: non-hardy shrub; requires a cool greenhouse and a well-drained, lime-free soil, great care must be taken with watering, not too much and not too little, the water must be lime-free; propagated by cuttings and by seed

EPACRISIS are the Heaths of Australasia, and, as they are often found growing on hilltops, the word *Epacris* was appositely coined from the Greek for 'on' and 'summit'. *E. purpurescens* is one of the best of the species. A shrub in the wild will grow to over a metre (3 feet) and have many flower spikes, though cultivated as a greenhouse plant for winter flowering in the northern hemisphere it will most probably have its spikes reduced to five. These bloom so prodigiously they require the support of stakes. Oddly, though dried specimens had been in Europe for years no *Epacris* was introduced into cultivation until one of Sir Joseph Banks's collectors sent seed of *C. purpurescens* in 1803. This collector, a Yorkshireman named George Caley, was not a favourite of Banks. As a boy he had written to the great Sir Joseph in London declaring he intended to be a botanist. With this defiant letter he sent a bundle of plants and because Banks found one or two that were new to him he gave the boy somewhat grudging encouragement, told him to go to Kew and earn ten shillings a week as a weeder and thus learn how to be useful. Caley promptly turned up in London and at the end of two years he announced he knew quite enough about plants and wished to be sent abroad. Banks was unaccustomed to bantam cocks in his roost and gave him a cold shoulder. He was busy at the time arranging the appointment of the notorious Captain Bligh of HMS *Bounty* fame as Governor of the run-down colony of New South Wales. Then he had second thoughts about Caley, decided he would feel easier in his mind if the blunt young man were at the antipodes, and so he was sent off to Australia with an introduction to Governor Bligh. The strange pair became friends, and Caley began to make huge collections and write equally huge descriptions of plants. An account of 318 closely written pages once accompanied 31 packets of seeds. He botanised in some of the loneliest places on earth and it began to get on his nerves. When not collecting he lived so riotously that even Bligh and Banks, both typical men of their day, were dismayed. Banks stopped his salary, but seeds and notes continued to pour in until one day Caley himself arrived in England. He was accompanied by an Aborigine. Fortuitously a Superintendent for the St. Vincent Botanic Garden was required and, most anxious to be rid of Caley, Banks arranged for him to be appointed. Even in the West Indies, though he behaved more circumspectly, Caley managed to cause offence. He closed the gardens on Sundays, a favourite visiting day, because, he declared openly, the quality helped themselves to cuttings.

Plate 120

Epacris purpureascens

INDEX OF PLANT NAMES

247

INDEX OF PLATES

Plate numbers marked (c) refer to the original English edition of
Curtis's Flower Garden Displayed

PLATE		SCIENTIFIC NAME	ENGLISH NAME
26	(c 239)	*Zephyranthes atamasco*	Atamasco Lily
27	(c 113)	*Ipomoea purpurea*	Purple Bindweed, Morning Glory
28	(c 357)	*Briza maxima*	Great Quaking Grass
29	(c 109)	*Lavatera trimestris*	Annual Lavatera
30	(c 246)	*Aquilegia canadensis*	Canadian Columbine
31	(c 245)	*Teucrium fruticans*	Shrubby Germander, Tree Germander
32	(c 931)	*Phytolacca americana*	Pokeweed, Pigeon-berry
33	(c 47)	*Sprekelia formosissima*	Jacobean Amaryllis, or Lily
34	(c 275)	*Liriodendron tulipifera*	Tulip Tree, Whitewood
35	(c 950)	*Arisaema triphyllum*	Jack-in-the-Pulpit
36	(c 500)	*Agapanthus africanus*	African Agapanthus, Blue Lily
37	(c 23)	*Tropaeolum majus*	Greater Indian Cress, Nasturtium
38	(c 279)	*Plumeria rubra*	Red Plumeria, Frangipani, West Indian Jasmine
39	(c 321)	*Cotyledon orbiculata*	Round-leaved Navel-wort, Pig's Ear
40	(c 444)	*Canaria canariensis*	Canary Bell-flower
41	(c 323)	*Rubus odoratus*	Flowering Raspberry, Thimbleberry
42	(c 60)	*Lathyrus odoratus*	Sweet Pea
43	(c 479)	*Tragopogon hybridus*	Goat's-beard, Smooth Geropogon
44	(c 339)	*Typhonium roxburghii*	Three-lobed Arum
45	(c 513)	*Aloe variegata*	Partridge-breasted Aloe, Tiger Aloe
46	(c 722)	*Trichosanthes anguina*	Snake-gourd, Viper-gourd, Serpent Cucumber
47	(c 29)	*Reseda odorata*	Sweet-scented Reseda, Mignonette
48	(c 131)	*Castesbaea spinosa*	Thorny Catesbaea, Lily Thorn
49	(c 526)	*Cornus florida*	Great-flowered Cornel, Flowering Dogwood
50	(c 628)	*Petrea racemosa*	Twining Petrea, Purple Wreath
51	(c 668)	*Gordonia lasianthus*	Loblolly Bay, Black Laurel
52	(c 12)	*Dodecatheon meadia*	Shooting Stars, Mead's Dodecatheon
53	(c 418)	*Watsonia meriana*	Watsonia
54	(c 780)	*Sarracenia flava*	Yellow Side-saddle Flower, Yellow Sarracenia
55	(c 662)	*Hypoxis stellata*	Yellow Star-hypoxis
56	(c 661)	*Crinum bulbispermum*	Long-leaved Crinum
57	(c 334)	*Hypericum chinense*	Chinese St. John's Wort
58	(c 676)	*Erinacea anthyllis*	Hedgehog Broom, Branch Thorn

PLATE		SCIENTIFIC NAME	ENGLISH NAME
59	(c 873)	*Hemerocallis minor*	Narrow-leaved Day Lily
60	(c 89)	*Viola pedata*	Bird's-foot Violet, Cut-leaved Violet, Crowfoot Violet
61	(c 40)	*Trillium sessile*	Sessile Trillium
62	(c 405)	*Lagerstroemia indica*	Indian Lilac, Crepe Myrtle
63	(c 534)	*Aristolochia macrophylla*	Dutchman's Pipe
64	(c 650)	*Rhododendron ponticum*	Purple Rhododendron
65	(c 920)	*Kaempfera rotunda*	
66	(c 196)	*Bergenia crassifolia*	Bergenia
67	(c 926)	*Paeonia tenuifolia*	Fine-leaved Paeony
68	(c 466)	*Chimonanthus praecox*	Japan Allspice
69	(c 577)	*Moraea tristis*	Moraea
70	(c 785)	*Dionaea muscipula*	Venus's Fly-trap
71	(c 998)	*Camellia sinensis*	Tea
72	(c 129)	*Hippeastrum vittatum*	Hippeastrum
73	(c 167)	*Sophora tetraptera*	Winged-podded Sophora, Kowhai
74	(c 302)	*Acacia myrtifolia*	Myrtle-leaved Mimosa
75	(c 640)	*Lonicera implexa*	Honeysuckle
76	(c 67)	*Aethephyllum pinnatifidum*	Jagged-leaved Fig-marigold
77	(c 385)	*Monsonia lobata*	Broad-leaved Monsonia
78	(c 326)	*Aridaria viridiflora*	Green Fig-marigold
79	(c 346)	*Protea repens*	Sugarbush
80	(c 119)	*Strelitzia reginae*	Bird of Paradise Flower, Bird's Tongue Flower
81	(c 690)	*Gardenia rothmannia*	Spotted Gardenia
82	(c 155)	*Oxalis versicolor*	Striped-flower'd Wood-sorrel
83	(c 56)	*Pelargonium glaucum*	Spear-leaved Geranium, Pelargonium
84	(c 549)	*Ixia viridiflora*	Green Ixia
85	(c 242)	*Hebe elliptica*	
86	(c 125)	*Alstromeria caryophyllaea*	Striped Alstromeria
87	(c 406)	*Senecio cruentus*	Purple-leaved Cineraria
88	(c 348)	*Calceolaria fothergillii*	Fothergill's Slipperwort
89	(c 39)	*Dianthus caryophyllus*	Bizarre Border Carnation
90	(c 376)	*Salvia leonuroides*	Shining Sage
91	(c 913)	*Eucomis punctata*	Spotted-leaved Eucomis
92	(c 367)	*Aloysia triphylla*	Lemon Verbena
93	(c 225)	*Centropogon cornutus*	
94	(c 460)	*Maurandya scandens*	Bastard Foxglove
95	(c 138)	*Kalmia hirsuta*	Hairy Mountain Laurel

PLATE		SCIENTIFIC NAME	ENGLISH NAME
96	(C 572)	*Epidendrum cochleatum*	Purple-flowered Epidendrum, Clam Flower
97	(C 819)	*Nymphaea odorata*	Sweet-scented Water-lily
98	(C 903)	*Nelumbo nucifera*	Sacred Lotus, Bean of India
99	(C 350)	*Erica ventricosa*	Porcelain Heath
100	(C 116)	*Calopogon pulchellus*	Pretty Calopogon, Grass-pink
101	(C 97)	*Fuchsia magellanica*	Fuchsia
102	(C 438)	*Hydrangea macrophylla*	Garden Hydrangea
103	(C 404)	*Campanula mollis*	Soft Bell-flower
104	(C 451)	*Blakea trinerva*	Jamaican Rose
105	(C 327)	*Chrysanthemum vestitum-indicum*	Autumn-flowering Chrysanthemum
106	(C 516)	*Sparmannia africana*	African Hemp
107	(C 620)	*Pterospermum acerifolium*	Maple-leaved Pterospermum
108	(C 390)	*Magnolia liliflora*	Purple Magnolia
109	(C 263)	*Hardenbergia violacea*	Purple Glycine
110	(C 325)	*Rhinacanthus nastulus*	Ringworm Root
111	(C 801)	*Billardiera scandens*	Apple-berry
112	(C 646)	*Cipura paludosa*	
113	(C 851)	*Cobaea scandens*	Climbing Cobaea, Cup-and-Saucer Plant
114	(C 769)	*Lagunaria patersonii*	Norfolk Island Hibiscus
115	(C 387)	*Cymbidium aloifolium*	
116	(C 582)	*Gladiolus cuspidatus*	
117	(C 786)	*Stapelia verrucosa*	Warty Carrion Flower
118	(C 705)	*Gentiana decumbens*	
119	(C 667)	*Zenobia pulverulenta*	
120	(C 844)	*Epacris purpurescens*	Rigid Epacris